ADAPTED FOR YOUNG ADULTS

JUST
MERCY

*A True Story of
the Fight for Justice*

ADAPTED FOR YOUNG ADULTS

JUST MERCY

*A True Story of
the Fight for Justice*

Bryan Stevenson

EMBER

Text copyright © 2018 by Bryan A. Stevenson
Motion Picture Artwork © 2019 Warner Bros. Entertainment Inc.

All rights reserved. Published in the United States by Ember, an imprint of Random House Children's Books, a division of Penguin Random House LLC, New York. Originally published in hardcover in the United States by Delacorte Press, an imprint of Random House Children's Books, a division of Penguin Random House LLC, New York, in 2018.

This work is based on *Just Mercy: A Story of Justice and Redemption,* copyright © 2014 by Bryan Stevenson. Published in hardcover in the United States by Spiegel & Grau, an imprint of Random House, a division of Penguin Random House LLC, New York, in 2014.

Ember and the E colophon are registered trademarks of Penguin Random House LLC.

Visit us on the Web! GetUnderlined.com

Educators and librarians, for a variety of teaching tools, visit us at RHTeachersLibrarians.com

The Library of Congress has cataloged the hardcover edition of this work as follows:
Names: Stevenson, Bryan, author.
Title: Just mercy : adapted for young adults : a true story of the fight for justice / Bryan A. Stevenson.
Description: New York : Delacorte Press, 2018.
Identifiers: LCCN 2018015248 (print) | LCCN 2018015359 (ebook) |
ISBN 978-0-525-58005-8 (ebook) | ISBN 978-0-525-58003-4 (hardback) |
ISBN 978-0-525-58004-1 (library binding)
Subjects: LCSH: Stevenson, Bryan—Juvenile literature. | Equal Justice Initiative—Juvenile literature. | Lawyers—United States—Biography—Juvenile literature. | Social reformers—United States—Biography—Juvenile literature. | Sentences (Criminal procedure)—United States—Juvenile literature. | Criminal justice, Administration of—United States—Juvenile literature. | Equality before the law—United States—Juvenile literature.
Classification: LCC KF373.S7435 (ebook) |
LCC KF373.S7435 A3 2018 (print) | DDC 340.092 [B]—dc23

ISBN 978-0-593-17704-4 (movie tie-in trade pbk.)

Printed in the United States of America
10 9 8 7 6 5 4 3 2 1

To all the young people
I've had the privilege
to represent

Love is the motive, but justice is the instrument.

—REINHOLD NIEBUHR

CONTENTS

ADAPTED FOR YOUNG ADULTS

JUST MERCY

*A True Story of
the Fight for Justice*

Higher Ground

I wasn't prepared to meet a condemned man. In 1983, I was a twenty-three-year-old Harvard Law School student working at an internship in Georgia, eager and worried that I was in over my head. I had never seen the inside of a maximum-security prison—and had certainly never been to death row.

Georgia's death row is in a prison outside of Jackson, a remote, rural town. I drove there by myself, my heart pounding harder the closer I got. I was convinced that this man was going to be very disappointed to see me. I didn't really know anything about capital punishment and hadn't even taken a class in criminal procedure yet. I didn't have a basic grasp of the complex appeals process that shaped death penalty litigation, a process that would in time become as familiar to me as the back of my hand.

I studied philosophy in college and didn't realize until my senior year that no one would pay me to philosophize when I graduated. I was uncertain about what I wanted to do with my life, but I knew it would have something to do with the lives of the poor, America's history of racial inequality, and the struggle to be just and fair with one another. I found two programs that seemed like the right fit: at Harvard, I could study law while also pursuing a graduate degree in public policy at the Kennedy School of Government.

Not long after classes began, I started to worry I'd made the wrong choice. I felt less experienced than my peers. I had never even met a lawyer before starting law school. I felt very fortunate to have been admitted, but by the end of my first year I'd grown disenchanted. Harvard Law School was a pretty intimidating place. And the courses seemed disconnected from the race and poverty issues that had motivated me to study the law in the first place.

While my classmates put on expensive suits and interviewed at firms in New York, Los Angeles, or Washington, DC, I spent the summer after my first year in law school working with a juvenile justice project in Philadelphia and taking advanced calculus courses at night to prepare for my next year at the Kennedy School. The public policy program's curriculum was extremely numbers and statistics focused, leaving me feeling adrift. Then, suddenly, everything came into focus.

I discovered that the law school offered a one-month intensive course on race and poverty litigation, taught by Betsy Bartholet, who had worked as an attorney with the NAACP Legal Defense Fund. Students were required to spend the month with an organization doing social justice work. So, in

December 1983, I found myself on a plane to Atlanta, Georgia, where I was scheduled to spend a few weeks working with the Southern Prisoners Defense Committee (SPDC, now known as the Southern Center for Human Rights or SCHR). Their mission? To defend condemned people on death row in Georgia.

I met Steve Bright, the director of the SPDC, on my flight down. Steve was a brilliant trial lawyer in his mid-thirties. He'd grown up on a farm in Kentucky, ended up in Washington, DC, at the Public Defender Service, and had just been recruited to take over the SPDC. Unlike so many of my law professors, there was no disconnect between what he did and what he believed in. When we met, he warmly wrapped me in a full-body hug, and then we started talking. We didn't stop till we'd reached Atlanta.

"Bryan," he said at some point during our short flight, "capital punishment means 'them without the capital get the punishment.' We can't help people on death row without help from people like you."

I processed what he meant: people without money, or capital, were the ones who were punished. I was taken aback by his immediate belief that I had something to offer. He broke down the issues with the death penalty simply but persuasively, and I hung on every word, completely engaged by his dedication and charisma. It was deeply affirming to meet someone whose work so powerfully animated his life.

"I just hope you're not expecting anything too fancy while you're here," he said.

"Oh, no," I assured him. "I'm grateful for the opportunity to work with you."

"Well, we live kind of simply, and the hours are pretty intense," he warned.

I quickly realized he wasn't kidding.

There were just a few attorneys working at the SPDC when I arrived that winter. In their thirties, men and women, black and white, these lawyers were prepared to fight for the rights of the condemned and those facing unjust treatment in jails and prisons.

After years of prohibition and delay, executions were again taking place in the Deep South. Most of SPDC's lawyers had come to Georgia in response to a growing crisis: death row prisoners couldn't get lawyers and were being denied their right to receive counsel for legal advice. There was a growing fear that people would be killed without ever having their cases reviewed by skilled counsel. Every day, we got frantic calls from people who had no legal assistance but whose execution dates were on the calendar and approaching fast. I'd never heard voices so desperate.

When I started my internship, everyone was extremely kind to me, and I felt immediately at home. I did clerical work, answering phones and researching legal questions for staff. I was just getting settled into my routine when Steve asked me to go to death row to meet with a condemned man who had been there for more than two years; my job was to convey to him one simple message: *You will not be killed in the next year.*

Driving through farmland in rural Georgia, I rehearsed what I would say when I met this man.

"Hello, my name is Bryan. I'm a student with the . . ." No. "I'm a law student with . . ." No. "My name is Bryan Stevenson. I'm a legal intern with the Southern Prisoners Defense Committee, and I've been instructed to inform you that you will not be executed soon." "You can't be executed soon." "You are not at risk of execution anytime soon." No.

Soon I found myself pulling up to the intimidating barbed-wire fence and white guard tower of the Georgia Diagnostic and Classification State Prison, or as we called it at SPDC, Jackson.

This was a hard place.

When I told the visitation officer that I was a paralegal sent to meet with a death row prisoner, he looked at me suspiciously. I waited until he brusquely directed me to the small room where the visit would take place. "Don't get lost in here; we don't promise to come and find you," he warned.

The visitation room was an empty metal cage. It was small, and although I knew it couldn't be true, it felt like it was getting smaller by the second. I began worrying again about my lack of preparation. I'd scheduled to meet with the client for one hour, but how would I fill all that time? I sat down on one of the stools that were bolted to the floor and waited anxiously. Finally, I heard the clanging of chains on the other side of the door.

The man who walked in seemed even more nervous than I was. He glanced at me, his face screwed up in a worried wince. He was a young, neatly groomed African American man with short hair—clean-shaven, medium frame and build—wearing bright, clean prison whites. He looked immediately familiar to me, like everyone I'd grown up with, friends from school, people I played sports or music with. The guard removed his handcuffs and the shackles around his ankles, and then locked eyes with me and told me I had one hour. The officer seemed to take pleasure in our discomfort, grinning at me before turning on his heel and leaving the room. The metal door banged loudly behind him.

The condemned man didn't come any closer, and I didn't know what else to do, so I walked over and offered him my hand. He shook it cautiously. We sat down and he spoke first.

"I'm Henry," he said.

"I'm very sorry" were the first words I blurted out. Despite all my preparations and rehearsed remarks, I couldn't stop myself from apologizing repeatedly.

"I'm really sorry, I'm really sorry, uh, okay, I don't really know, uh, I'm just a law student, I'm not a real lawyer. . . . I'm so sorry I can't tell you very much, but I don't know very much."

The man looked at me worriedly. "Is everything all right with my case?"

"Oh, yes, sir. The lawyers at SPDC sent me down to tell you that they don't have a lawyer yet . . . but you're not at risk of execution anytime in the next year. . . . We're working on finding you a lawyer, a real lawyer, and we hope the lawyer will be down to see you in the next few months. I'm just a law student. I'm really happy to help, I mean, if there's something I can do."

The man interrupted my chatter by quickly grabbing my hands.

"I'm not going to have an execution date anytime in the next year?"

"No, sir. They said it would be at least a year before you get an execution date." Those words didn't sound very comforting to me. But Henry just squeezed my hands tighter and tighter.

"Thank you, man. I mean, really, thank you! This is great news." His shoulders relaxed, and he looked at me with intense relief in his eyes.

"You are the first person I've met in over two years after coming to death row who is not another death row prisoner or a death row guard. I'm so glad you're here, and I'm so glad to get this news." He exhaled loudly.

"I've been talking to my wife on the phone, but I haven't wanted her to come and visit me or bring the kids because I was afraid they'd show up and I'd have an execution date.

I just don't want them here like that. Now I'm going to tell them they can come and visit. Thank you!"

I was astonished that he was so happy. I relaxed, too, and soon we were both lost in conversation. He told me about his trial; I answered his questions about law school. We talked about our families, about music, about prison. We talked about what's important in life and what's not. We laughed at times, and there were moments when he was very emotional and sad. We kept talking and talking, and it was only when I heard a loud bang on the door that I realized I'd stayed way past my allotted time for the legal visit. I looked at my watch. I'd been there three hours.

The guard came in. He snarled at me, "You should have been done a long time ago. You have to leave."

He pulled Henry's hands together behind his back and locked them in handcuffs. Then he roughly shackled Henry's ankles. I could see Henry grimacing with pain.

I said, "I think those cuffs are on too tight. Can you loosen them, please?"

"You don't tell me how to do my job."

Henry gave me a smile and said, "It's okay, Bryan. Don't worry about this. Just come back and see me again, okay?" I could see him wince with each click of the chains being tightened around his waist.

Distraught, I mumbled, "I'm really sorry. I'm really sor—"

"Don't worry about this, Bryan," he said, cutting me off. "Just come back."

I wanted to say something reassuring, something that expressed my gratitude to him for being so patient with me and my nerves. But I couldn't think of anything. As the guard shoved him roughly toward the door, Henry looked back at me and smiled. Just before he could be pushed out the door, he planted his feet on the floor. Then he did something completely unexpected. He closed his eyes and tilted his head back. I was confused by what he was doing, but then, as he opened his mouth, I understood. He began to sing. He had a tremendous baritone voice that was strong and clear. It startled both me and the guard, who stopped his pushing.

> *I'm pressing on, the upward way*
> *New heights I'm gaining, every day*
> *Still praying as, I'm onward bound*
> *Lord, plant my feet on Higher Ground.*

It was an old hymn they used to sing all the time in the church where I grew up. I hadn't heard it in years. Henry sang slowly and with great sincerity and conviction. Because his ankles were shackled and his hands were locked behind his back, Henry almost stumbled when the guard shoved him forward again—but he kept on singing down the hall.

Hearing his song was a precious gift. I had come into the prison feeling insecure and inadequate. I had no right to expect anything from a condemned man on death row. Yet he gave me an astonishing measure of his humanity and compassion.

In that moment, Henry altered something in my understanding of human potential, redemption, and hopefulness.

I finished my internship, committed to helping the death row prisoners I had met that month. Once I returned to law school, I felt an intense desire to understand the laws that permitted and sanctioned the death penalty and other extreme punishments. I piled up courses: constitutional law, litigation, appellate procedure, and federal courts. I plunged deeply into the history of race, poverty, and power. Both law school and my public policy degree had seemed abstract and disconnected before, but after meeting the desperate and imprisoned, they both became relevant and critically important.

My short time on death row revealed that there was something skewed in the way our judicial system interprets the law. The more I reflected on the experience, the more I recognized that I had been struggling my whole life with the question of how and why some people are judged unfairly.

I grew up in a poor, rural settlement on the eastern shore of the Delmarva Peninsula, in Delaware, where the racial history of this country casts a long shadow. Confederate flags, symbols of white supremacy and slavery, were proudly displayed throughout the region.

African Americans lived in racially segregated ghettos isolated by railroad tracks within small towns or in "colored sections" in the country. Some people lived in tiny shacks;

families without indoor plumbing had to use outhouses. We shared our outdoor play space with chickens and pigs.

The black people around me were strong and determined but marginalized and excluded. My father left the area as a teenager because there was no local high school for black children. He returned with my mother and found work in a food factory; on weekends he did domestic work at beach cottages and rentals. My mother worked at an Air Force base.

My relatives worked hard all the time but never seemed to prosper. My grandmother was the daughter of people who were enslaved in Caroline County, Virginia. She was born in the 1880s, her parents in the 1840s. Her father talked to her all the time about growing up in slavery. He had learned to read and write but kept it a secret—until Emancipation, that is, when he was freed. The legacy of slavery shaped my grandmother. It shaped the way she raised her nine children. It influenced the way she talked to me, the way she constantly told me, "Keep close."

When I visited her, she would hug me so tightly that I could barely breathe, but it made me happy to be wrapped in her formidable arms. "You can't understand most of the important things from a distance, Bryan. You have to get close," she told me often.

The distance I experienced in my first year of law school made me feel lost. Closeness to the condemned, to people unfairly judged, that was what guided me back to something that felt like home.

This book is about how quickly we condemn people in this country. It is about the dramatic increase in the number of people incarcerated in America—a phenomenon known as mass incarceration. It is about extreme punishment—the harsh, excessive sentences we give to the condemned, and the sinister treatment they face once in prison. It is about how we create injustice by allowing our fear, anger, and distance to guide the way we treat those who are more vulnerable. It's also about a dramatic period in our recent history that marked the lives of millions of Americans—of all races, ages, and genders—and the country as a whole.

When I first visited death row in December 1983, America was going through a radical transformation: we were imprisoning more people than any other country. Today we have the highest rate of incarceration in the world. In the early 1970s, the prison population was 300,000 people; currently, it's 2.3 million people. Nearly 6 million people are on probation (meaning, they've been released from their prison sentence but are still supervised) or on parole (meaning, they've been released from their prison sentence on "good behavior"). One in every fifteen people born in the United States in 2001 is expected to go to jail or prison; one in every three black male babies born in this century is expected to be incarcerated. To be clear, these numbers reflect who is being convicted and incarcerated, *not* who is necessarily committing crimes.

We have shot, hanged, gassed, electrocuted, and lethally injected hundreds of people in the name of the law. Thousands more await their execution in the section of prisons known as death row. We've sent a quarter million kids, some under the age of twelve, to adult jails and prisons. For years, we've been the only country in the world that condemns children to life imprisonment without parole.

We've created laws that make nonviolent offenses—like writing a bad check or committing a petty theft—result in life imprisonment. We have locked away people with substance abuse problems, with more than a half million people in state or federal prisons for drug offenses.

We've given up on rehabilitation, education, and services for the imprisoned because providing assistance to the incarcerated is apparently too kind and compassionate. We've institutionalized policies that reduce people to their worst acts and permanently label them "criminal," "murderer," "rapist," "thief," "drug dealer," "sex offender," "felon"—identities they cannot change regardless of the circumstances of their crimes or any improvements they might try making in their lives.

Mass incarceration's effects on the world outside of prisons have been equally profound. We ban poor people and their children from receiving food stamps and public housing if they have prior drug convictions—often leaving them homeless and unemployable. Some states strip people with criminal convictions of the right to vote; as a result, in several Southern states, disenfranchisement among African American men has reached levels unseen since before the Voting Rights Act of 1965, which legally prohibited racial discrimination in voting.

We also make terrible mistakes. Thousands of innocent people suffer in prison. Scores have been exonerated (cleared of guilt) after being sentenced to death and nearly executed. Hundreds of prisoners who are not on death row have been released after being proved innocent through DNA testing. Presumptions of guilt based on poverty and racial bias have created a system that is defined by error.

Finally, we spend lots of money on prisons, nearly $80 billion every year. To cover the cost, state governments have taken away funds from public services, education, health, and welfare. In fact, private prison builders and prison service companies have paid millions of dollars to state and local governments, trying to convince them to create *new* crimes, impose harsher sentences, and keep more people locked up so that *they* can increase profits. The privatization of mass incarceration is a moneymaker for a few and a costly nightmare for the rest of us—and it has ruined efforts to improve public safety, reduce the costs of mass incarceration, and most significantly, promote rehabilitation of the incarcerated.

After graduating from law school, I returned to the Deep South to represent the poor, the incarcerated, and the condemned. In the last thirty years, I've gotten close to people who have been wrongly convicted and sent to death row, people like Walter

McMillian. In this book you will learn the story of Walter's case, which shows how our legal system convicts and condemns people irresponsibly—with disturbing and traumatic results. But Walter's case also taught me something else: there is light within this darkness.

Walter's story is one of many that I tell in these chapters. I've represented abused and neglected children who were prosecuted as adults and suffered more abuse and mistreatment after being placed in adult facilities. I've represented women, whose numbers in prison have increased 640 percent in the last thirty years, and seen how our hysteria about drug addiction and our hostility to the poor have made us quick to criminalize them. I've represented mentally disabled people whose illnesses have landed them in prison for decades. I've gotten close to victims of violent crime and their families, and witnessed how mass imprisonment has even made prison staff more violent and angry, and less just and merciful.

I've also represented people who have committed terrible crimes but nonetheless strive to recover and to find redemption. I have discovered, deep in the hearts of many condemned and incarcerated people, seeds of hope and humanity that come to astonishing life when nurtured by very simple acts of care and respect.

My work has taught me a vital lesson: *Each of us is more than the worst thing we've ever done.* I am persuaded that the opposite of poverty is not wealth; the opposite of poverty is justice. Finally, I've come to believe that the true measure of our commitment to justice, fairness, and equality cannot be measured by how we treat the rich, the respected, and the privileged among us. The true measure of our character is how we treat the poor, the disfavored, the accused, the incarcerated, and the condemned.

We are all implicated when we allow other people to be mistreated. An absence of compassion can corrupt the decency of a community, a state, an entire nation. Fear and anger can make us cruel and abusive. We all suffer from the absence of mercy and we harm ourselves as much as we victimize others. The closer we get to mass incarceration and extreme levels of punishment, the more I believe it's necessary to recognize that we all need mercy, we all need justice, and—perhaps— we all need some measure of unmerited grace.

CHAPTER ONE

Mockingbird Players

I was in my late twenties and about to start my fourth year at the Southern Prisoners Defense Committee (SPDC) when I met Walter McMillian. His case was one of the many I was trying frantically to keep up with. After all, a crisis was growing: Alabama had no public defender system, which meant that many death row prisoners didn't have lawyers to represent them.

My friend Eva Ansley was at an Alabama prison project to track cases and match lawyers to prisoners. In 1988, we got federal funding to create a legal center that could represent people on death row. I'd already worked on lots of death penalty cases in several Southern states, sometimes winning a stay, which puts a stop to the execution, just minutes before an electrocution was scheduled.

When I'd last visited death row, I met with five desperate condemned men: Willie Tabb, Vernon Madison, Jesse Morrison, Harry Nicks, and Walter McMillian. The most memorable thing about Walter was how insistent he was that he'd been wrongly convicted.

"Mr. Bryan, I know it may not matter to you, but it's important to me that you know that I'm innocent and didn't do what they said I did, not no kinda way," he told me in the meeting room. His voice was level but laced with emotion. I nodded. I had learned to accept what clients tell me until the facts suggest something else.

"I'm sure I'm not the first person on death row to tell you that they're innocent, but I really need you to believe me. My life has been ruined! This lie they put on me is more than I can bear, and if I don't get help from someone who believes me—"

His lip began to quiver, and he clenched his fists to stop himself from crying.

"I'm sorry, I know you'll do everything you can to help me," he said, his voice quieter. My instinct was to comfort him; his pain seemed so sincere. There wasn't much I could do, but I reassured him that I would look at everything carefully.

Back at the office, I went through the mound of records until I found the transcripts from Walter McMillian's trial. The trial had been short. I started reading.

Walter McMillian was at least fifteen years older than me, not particularly well educated, and he hailed from a small rural community. Though he had lived in Monroe County his whole life, he had never heard of the author Harper Lee—also a

Monroeville, Alabama, native—or her award-winning novel *To Kill a Mockingbird.*

Mockingbird tells the story of an innocent black man who is accused of raping a white woman in the 1930s, and is bravely defended by Atticus Finch, a white lawyer. What is often overlooked is that the black man falsely accused in the story was not *successfully* defended by Atticus. Tom Robinson, the wrongly accused black defendant, is found guilty. Later he dies when, full of despair, he makes a desperate attempt to escape from prison. He is shot seventeen times in the back by his captors. While the novel captivated millions of readers—and confronted them with some of the realities of race and justice in the South—its harder truths did not take root.

Walter McMillian, like the character Tom Robinson, grew up in one of several poor black settlements outside of Monroeville, where he worked the fields with his family before he was old enough to attend school. Educational opportunities for black children in the 1950s were limited, but Walter's mother got him to the dilapidated "colored school" for a couple of years when he was young. By the time he was eight or nine, though, he became too valuable for "plowin', plantin', and pickin'" cotton to justify the remote advantages of continuing school.

Some backstory about Walter's hometown: Monroe County had been developed by plantation owners in the nineteenth century for the production of cotton. The fertile, rich black soil of the area attracted white settlers from the Carolinas, who amassed plantations and a huge slave population. Even decades after the Civil War and Emancipation, the African American population toiled in the fields of the "Black Belt" as sharecroppers and tenant farmers, dependent on white landowners for survival.

By the 1950s, small cotton farming was replaced with timber farming as Alabama's thriving industry. White landowners opened pulp and paper mills across the region. Acres and acres of land were converted to growing pine trees for paper mills and industrial uses.

Times were changing—for better and for worse. African Americans, largely excluded from this new paper industry, found themselves confronting new economic challenges even as they won basic civil rights. The brutal era of sharecropping and Jim Crow was ending, but what followed was persistent unemployment and worsening poverty. The region's counties remained some of the poorest in America.

Walter started his own pulpwood business in the 1970s. He smartly—and bravely—borrowed money to buy his own power saw, tractor, and pulpwood truck. By the 1980s, he had developed a solid business that didn't make much extra money but afforded him something else he valued: independence. If he had worked at the mill or the factory—the kind of job that most poor black Alabamans worked—it would mean working for white business owners and dealing with the racial stress that that implied in 1970s and 1980s Alabama. Walter couldn't escape the reality of racism, but having his own business gave him a flexibility that many African Americans did not enjoy.

Walter's independence won him respect and admiration, but it also sparked contempt and suspicion. His freedom was, to some of the white people in town, well beyond what African Americans with limited education could achieve through legitimate means. Still, he was pleasant, respectful, generous, and accommodating, which made him well liked by the people—black or white—with whom he did business.

Like anyone, Walter had his flaws. Though he and his wife, Minnie, had three children, it was well known that he was romantically involved with other women. "Tree work" is notoriously demanding and dangerous. With few ordinary comforts in his life, the attention of women was something Walter did not easily resist. There was something about his rugged exterior—his long, bushy hair and uneven beard—combined with his generous and charming nature that attracted the attention of some women.

Walter grew up understanding that it was forbidden for a black man to be intimate with a white woman. He didn't initially think much of the flirtations of Karen Kelly, a young white woman he'd met at the Waffle House where he ate breakfast. She was attractive, but he didn't take her too seriously. When her flirtations became more explicit, Walter hesitated, and then persuaded himself that no one would know.

After a few weeks, it became clear that his relationship with

Karen was trouble. She was younger and married. As word got around that the two were "friends," she seemed to take a mischievous pride in her intimacy with Walter. When her husband, Joe, found out, things quickly turned ugly. Karen and Joe had been unhappy and were already planning to divorce. Now, Joe was threatening to take custody of their children—and to "disgrace" her by exposing her relationship with a black man.

Soon enough, Walter received a subpoena summoning him to testify at a hearing about the Kellys' custody battle. He knew it was going to cause him serious problems. Nervously, he went to the courthouse. When Walter took the stand, the lawyer for Joe Kelly's husband asked him crude, hostile questions. Walter wanted to forget about the whole ordeal, but word of the interracial affair spread quickly, and his reputation shifted. No longer the hardworking pulpwood man, known to white people almost exclusively for what he could do with a saw in the pine trees, Walter now represented something more threatening in their eyes.

Fears of interracial sex and marriage have deep roots in the United States. In the aftermath of slavery, the creation of a system of racial hierarchy and segregation was largely designed to prevent relationships like Walter and Karen's. In fact, interracial relationships were legally prohibited by "antimiscegenation statutes" (the word *miscegenation* came into use in the 1860s, when supporters of slavery coined the term to promote the fear of interracial sex and marriage and the race mixing that would result if slavery was abolished). For over a century, many Southern law enforcement officials saw it as part of their duty to punish black men who had been intimate with "their" white women.

The federal government had promised racial equality to freed former slaves during the short period of Reconstruction. But after federal troops left Alabama in the 1870s, white supremacy swiftly returned, and a series of racially restrictive laws enforced the subordination of African Americans. Voting rights were taken away. Interracial sex and marriage were criminalized, and states throughout the South used the anti-miscegenation laws to justify the forced sterilization of poor and minority women. Forbidding sex between white women and black men became an intense preoccupation throughout the South.

In 1882, the Alabama Supreme Court reviewed a case regarding an affair between Tony Pace, an African American man, and Mary Cox, a white woman. Both received prison terms. The following year, the United States Supreme Court reviewed the Alabama court's decision. Using "separate but equal" language—just as the *Plessy v. Ferguson* case would, twenty years later—the court unanimously upheld Alabama's ban on interracial sex and marriage. Following the court's decision, many Southern and Midwestern states passed "racial integrity" laws that made it illegal for African Americans, and sometimes Native Americans and Asian Americans, to marry or have sex with white people.

It wasn't until 1967 that the US Supreme Court finally struck down anti-miscegenation statutes in *Loving v. Virginia,* but restrictions on interracial marriage persisted even after that landmark ruling. It was only in 2000 that the issue got on Alabama's statewide ballot, where a majority of voters chose to eliminate the ban—although 41 percent still voted to keep it.

Occasionally drinking too much, getting into a fight, or even having an extramarital affair—these slipups weren't significant enough to destroy the reputation and standing of an honest and industrious black man. But interracial dating, particularly with a married white woman, was for many whites a transgression in its own unique category of danger—with correspondingly extreme punishments. Hundreds of black men have been lynched for even unsubstantiated suggestions of such intimacy.

Walter may not have known the legal history, but like every black man in Alabama, he knew deep in his bones the perils of interracial romance for black men. Nearly a dozen people had been lynched in Monroe County, and dozens of additional lynchings had taken place in neighboring counties. These lynchings were acts of terror, inspiring fear that any encounter with a white person, any social misstep, any unintended slight, any ill-advised look or comment, could trigger a gruesome, even deadly, attack.

Walter heard his parents and relatives talk about lynchings when he was a young child. When he was twelve, the body of Russell Charley, a black man from Monroe County who was reputed to have had an interracial romance, was found hanging from a tree in Vredenburgh, Alabama. Walter remembered well the terror that shot through the black community in Monroe County when Charley's lifeless, bullet-ridden body was found swinging in a tree.

And now it seemed to Walter that everyone in Monroe County was talking about his own relationship with Karen Kelly. It worried him in a way that few things ever had.

A few weeks later, an even more unthinkable act shocked Monroeville. In the late morning of November 1, 1986, Ronda Morrison, a white, eighteen-year-old college student, and the beautiful young daughter of a respected local family, was found shot dead on the floor of Monroe Cleaners, the shop where she had worked.

Murder was uncommon in Monroeville. The death of young Ronda was a crime unlike anything the community had ever experienced. She was popular, an only child, and the kind of girl whom the entire white community embraced as a daughter.

The police initially believed that no one from the community, black or white, would have done something so horrific.

They pursued two Latino men who had been spotted in

Monroeville looking for work the day Ronda Morrison's body was found. Police tracked the suspects down in Florida but found that they could not have committed the murder. The former owner of the cleaners, an older white man named Miles Jackson, fell under suspicion, but there was no evidence that pointed to him as a killer. The current owner of the cleaners, Rick Blair, was questioned but considered an unlikely suspect. Within a few weeks, the police had tapped out their leads.

People in Monroe County began to whisper about the incompetence of the police. Why couldn't they even find a suspect? people murmured. Tom Tate was elected the new county sheriff days after the murder took place, and folks started to question whether he was up to the job. After all, a murderer was on the loose.

Meanwhile, Walter was wrestling with his own problems. He had been trying to end his relationship with Karen Kelly. The child custody proceedings and public scandal had taken a toll on her; she had started using drugs and seemed to fall apart. She began to associate with Ralph Myers, a white man with a badly disfigured face and lengthy criminal record. The relationship with Myers brought Karen to rock bottom. Together they became involved in dealing drugs. They were also implicated in another surprising crime: the murder of Vickie Lynn Pittman, a young woman from neighboring Escambia County.

While the death of Vickie Pittman was news, it failed to compare with the continuing mystery surrounding the death of Ronda Morrison. Vickie came from a poor white family, several of whose members were incarcerated. It was as if her lower social standing caused her life—and her death—to be seen as less valuable than Ronda Morrison's.

Police quickly concluded that Ralph Myers had been involved in the Pittman murder. When the police interrogated him, they encountered a man as psychologically complicated as he was physically scarred. Emotional and frail, Ralph craved attention—his skills lay in manipulation and misdirection. He believed that everything he said had to be epic, shocking, and elaborate. As a child living in foster care, he had been horribly burned in a fire. The burns so scarred and disfigured his face and neck that he needed multiple surgeries to regain basic functioning. He'd grown used to strangers staring and wincing at his scars. He was a tragic outcast who lived on the margins. So he tried to compensate by pretending to have inside knowledge about all sorts of mysteries.

Myers eventually admitted that he may have played an accidental role in Pittman's death, but quickly put the blame for the murder itself on others. The more he talked, the less believable his stories sounded. Officials began to suspect that Myers was the *only* killer and was desperately trying to cover his tracks.

Ralph Myers was illiterate, but he knew it was the Morrison crime that was preoccupying investigators. He changed his story again. This time, he told investigators that he *had* been involved in the murder of Vickie Pittman along with Karen Kelly—and her black boyfriend, Walter McMillian. But that wasn't all. He also told police that McMillian was responsible for the murder of *Ronda Morrison,* too.

That assertion got the attention of law enforcement officials, who were eager to pin the murder on *someone.* To see whether Ralph Myers and Walter McMillian were actually in cahoots, an ABI (Alabama Bureau of Investigation) agent asked Myers to meet Mr. McMillian at a store. Agents would monitor the encounter, watching from afar; the test would be whether the two men recognized each other.

Once Myers entered the store, he was not able to identify Walter McMillian—he had to ask the owner of the store to point Mr. McMillian out. He then delivered a note to Mr. McMillian, supposedly written by Karen Kelly. According to witnesses, Walter seemed confused both by Myers, a man he had never seen before, and the note itself. Walter threw the note away and went back to what he was doing. He paid little attention to the whole odd encounter.

The ABI agents were left with plenty of evidence indicating that the two men had never met, let alone committed murders together. Still, they persisted with the McMillian theory. Time was passing—seven months, by now—and the community was fearful and angry. They desperately needed an arrest.

Monroe County sheriff Tom Tate did not have much law enforcement experience. Now, four months into his term as sheriff, he faced a seemingly unsolvable murder and intense public pressure. But there was no evidence against Mr. McMillian—no evidence except that he was an African American man involved in an adulterous interracial affair, which meant he was reckless and possibly dangerous, even if he had no prior criminal history and a good reputation. Maybe that was evidence enough.

CHAPTER TWO

Stand

My $14,000 annual salary didn't leave me with much money for rent in Atlanta, so Steve Bright kindly took me in. Each day we dissected big and small issues from morning until midnight. I loved learning from him. After spending the first year and a half of my legal career sleeping on his living room couch, though, it was time to find an apartment of my own. When a law school classmate, Charles Bliss, moved to Atlanta, we realized we could pool our tiny salaries and afford a low-rent apartment. He was a white kid from North Carolina whom I'd grown close to in school. When work and lessons got overwhelming, we'd frequently retreat to the school gym to play basketball and to try to make sense of it all.

Eventually, Charlie and I shared a two-bedroom apartment in Midtown Atlanta. Because of my growing caseload in Alabama, I didn't get to spend much time there. My plan for a new law project to represent people on death row in Alabama was starting to take shape. My hope was to get the project off the ground in Alabama and eventually return to Atlanta to live. My docket of new death penalty cases in Alabama meant I was working insane hours driving back and forth and simultaneously trying to resolve several prison-condition cases.

Conditions of confinement for prisoners were getting worse everywhere. In the 1970s, the Attica prison riots drew national attention to horrible prison abuses. Inmates took over the Attica Correctional Facility, and news coverage of the revolt exposed Americans to the cruel practices within prisons. In solitary confinement, for example, inmates would be isolated in a small confined space for weeks or months at a time. Prisoners in some facilities would be placed in a "sweatbox," a casket-size hole or a box situated where the inmate would be forced to endure extreme heat for days or weeks. Some prisoners were tortured with electric cattle prods as punishment for violations of the prison's rule. Inmates at some facilities would be chained to "hitching posts," their arms fastened above their heads in a painful position in which they'd be forced to stand for hours. The practice, which wasn't declared unconstitutional until 2002, was one of many degrading and dangerous punishments imposed on incarcerated people. Terrible food and living conditions were widespread.

We were getting scores of letters from prisoners who continued to report horrible conditions. Prisoners reported that they were still being beaten by correctional staff and subjected to degrading punishments. An alarming number of cases came to us involving prisoners who had been found dead in their cells.

I was working on several of these cases, including one in Gadsden, Alabama, where jail officials claimed that a thirty-nine-year-old black man had died of natural causes after being arrested for traffic violations. His family maintained that he was beaten by police and jail officials who then denied him his asthma inhaler and medication despite his begging for it. I'd spent a lot of time with the grief-stricken family of Lourida Ruffin and heard what an affectionate father he had been, how kind he had been, and how people had made cruel assumptions about him because he was a black man at six feet five inches tall and over 250 pounds. His wife and mother recalled how sweet and gentle he had been.

Gadsden police had stopped Mr. Ruffin one night because they said his car was swerving. Police discovered that his license had expired a few weeks earlier, so he was taken into custody. When he arrived at the city jail badly bruised and bleeding, Mr. Ruffin told the other inmates that he had been beaten terribly and was desperately in need of his inhaler and asthma medication. When I started investigating the case, inmates at the jail told me they saw officers beating Mr. Ruffin before taking him to an isolation cell. Several hours later they saw medical personnel remove his body from the cell on a gurney.

Despite the reforms of the 1970s and early 1980s, inmate

death in jails and prisons was still a serious problem. Suicide, prisoner-on-prisoner violence, inadequate medical care, staff abuse, and guard violence claimed the lives of hundreds of prisoners every year.

I soon received other complaints from people in the Gadsden community. The parents of a black teenager who had been shot and killed by police told me that their son had been stopped for a minor traffic violation after running a red light. Their young son had just started driving and became very nervous when the police officer approached him. His family maintained that he reached down to the floor where he kept his gym bag to retrieve his newly issued driver's license. The police claimed he was reaching for a weapon—no weapon was found—and the teen was shot dead while he sat in his car. The officer who shot the boy said that the teen had been menacing and had moved quickly, in a threatening manner. The child's parents told me their son *was* generally nervous and easily frightened but was also obedient, very religious, and a good student. He would never have hurt anyone. The family persuaded civil rights leaders to push for an investigation into his death. Their pleas reached our office, and I was looking into the case along with the jail and prison cases.

Figuring out Alabama civil and criminal law while managing death penalty cases in several other states kept me very busy with long-distance driving and extremely long hours. My weathered 1975 Honda Civic was struggling to keep up. The radio had stopped working consistently a year earlier; it would come to life only if I hit a pothole or stopped suddenly enough to shake the car and spark a connection.

After I made the three-hour drive back from Gadsden early one day and heading straight to the office, it was once again approaching midnight as I left the office for home. I got in my car, and to my delight the radio came on as soon as I turned the ignition. It was a small thing, but it made my day. Better yet, the station was playing a retrospective on the music of Sly and the Family Stone. I'd grown up listening to Sly and found myself rolling joyfully through the streets of Atlanta to tunes like "Dance to the Music" and "Family Affair."

Our Midtown Atlanta apartment was on a dense residential street. Tonight, I was lucky: I found a parking spot steps from our new front door just as Sly was starting "Hot Fun in the Summertime." I needed to get to bed, but the moment was too good to let pass, so I remained in the car listening. Each time a tune ended, I told myself to go inside, but then another irresistible song would begin, and I would find myself unable to leave. "Stand!" the soaring Sly anthem with the great gospel-themed ending, was playing when I saw a flashing police light approaching.

Our section of the street ran only one way. My parked car was facing in the proper direction; the police car had come down the street in the wrong direction. I noticed for the first time that it wasn't an ordinary police cruiser but one of the special Atlanta SWAT cars. The officers had a spotlight attached to their vehicle, and they directed it at me sitting in my car. Only then did it occur to me that they might be there for me, but I couldn't imagine why. I had been parked on the street for about fifteen minutes listening to Sly. Only one of my car speakers worked, and not very well. I knew the music was quiet.

The officers sat there with their light pointed at me for a minute or so. I turned off the radio. I had case files on my car seat about Lourida Ruffin and the young man who had been shot in Gadsden. Eventually, two police officers got out of their vehicle. I noticed immediately that they weren't wearing the standard Atlanta police uniform. Instead, they were ominously dressed in military style black boots with black pants and vests.

It was time to get out of my car and go home. As soon as I opened the door and got out, the police officer who had started walking toward my vehicle drew his weapon and pointed it at me. My first instinct was to run. I quickly decided that wouldn't be smart. I must have looked completely bewildered.

"Move and I'll blow your head off!" The officer shouted the words, but I couldn't make any sense of them. I tried to stay calm; it was the first time in my life anyone had ever pointed a gun at me.

"Put your hands up!" The officer was a white man about my height. In the darkness, I could only make out his black uniform and his pointed weapon.

I put my hands up and noticed that he seemed nervous. I don't remember deciding to speak, I just remember the words coming out: "It's all right. It's okay."

I'm sure I sounded afraid because I was terrified. I kept saying the words over and over again. "It's okay, it's okay." Finally, I said, "I live here, this is my apartment."

I looked at the officer who was pointing the gun at my head less than fifteen feet away. I thought I saw his hands shaking. I kept saying as calmly as I could: "It's okay, it's okay."

The second officer, who had not drawn his weapon, inched cautiously toward me. He circled behind my parked car and came up behind me. He grabbed me by the arms and pushed me up against the back of my car. The other officer then lowered his weapon.

"What are you doing out here?" said the second officer, who seemed older than the one who had drawn his weapon. He sounded angry.

"I live here. I moved into that house down the street just a few months ago. My roommate is inside. You can go ask him." I hated how afraid I sounded and the way my voice was shaking.

"What are you doing out in the street?"

"I was just listening to the radio." He placed my hands on the car and bent me over the back of the vehicle. The SWAT car's bright spotlight shone on me. I noticed people up the block turning on their lights and peering outside. The house next to ours came to life, and a middle-aged white couple walked outside and stared.

The officer holding me asked me for my driver's license but wouldn't let me move my arms to retrieve it. I told him that it was in my back pocket, and he fished my wallet from my pants. The other officer was now leaning inside my car and going through my papers. I knew that he was conducting an illegal search. I was about to say something when I saw him open the glove compartment. Opening objects in a parked vehicle was so incredibly illegal that I realized he wasn't paying any attention to the rules, so saying something about it would be pointless.

There was nothing interesting in my car. No drugs, no alcohol, not even tobacco. I kept a giant-size bag of peanut M&M's and Bazooka bubble gum in the glove compartment to help stave off hunger when I didn't have time for a meal. There were just a few M&M's left in the bag, which the officer inspected carefully. He put his nose into the bag before tossing it back. I wouldn't be eating those M&M's.

I had not lived at our new address long enough to get a new driver's license, so the address on my license didn't match the new location. There was no legal requirement to update the driver's license, but it prompted the officer to hold me there for another ten minutes while he went back to his car to run a search on me. Even though it was late, neighbors were coming out of their homes to watch and comment. One older white woman loudly demanded that I be questioned about items she was missing: "Ask him about my radio and my vacuum cleaner!"

I kept hoping that my apartment light would come on and that Charlie would walk outside and help me out, but it occurred to me he might be at his girlfriend's place.

Finally, the officer returned and spoke to his partner: "They don't have anything on him." He sounded disappointed.

I found my nerve and took my hands off the car. "This is so messed up. I live here. You shouldn't have done this. Why did you do this?"

The older officer frowned at me. "Someone called about a suspected burglar. There have been a lot of burglaries in this neighborhood." Then he grinned. "We're going to let you go. You should be happy," he said.

With that, they got in their SWAT car and drove off. The neighbors looked me over one last time before retreating back into their homes.

I gathered up my papers, which the cop had scattered all over the car and onto the sidewalk. I unhappily threw my M&M's into a trash can on the street and then walked into my apartment. To my great relief, Charlie was there. I woke him to tell the story.

"They never even apologized," I kept saying. Charlie shared my outrage but soon fell back asleep. I couldn't sleep at all.

When I told Steve about the incident, he was furious and urged me to file a complaint with the Atlanta Police Department. Some folks said I should explain that I was a civil rights attorney working on police misconduct cases. But why, I wondered, should someone have to explain their professional credentials in order to be taken seriously about police misconduct?

I started writing my complaint to the Atlanta Police Department, determined not to reveal that I was an attorney. I detailed all of my concerns. I found Bureau of Justice Statistics reports that black men were eight times more likely to be killed by the police than whites. The problem would get worse as some states passed "Stand Your Ground" laws empowering armed citizens—who weren't even trained—to use lethal force as well.

Before I knew it, I had typed close to nine pages outlining all the things I thought had gone wrong. For two pages I detailed the completely illegal search of the vehicle and the absence of probable cause. I even cited about a half-dozen cases. I read over the complaint and realized that I had done everything but say, "I'm a lawyer."

I filed my complaint with the police department and tried to forget about the incident, but I couldn't. What bothered me most was the moment when the officer drew his weapon and I thought about running. I was a twenty-eight-year-old lawyer who had worked on police misconduct cases and knew to speak calmly to the officer when he threatened to shoot me.

When I thought about what I would have done when I was sixteen years old or nineteen or even twenty-four, I was scared to realize that *I* might have run. The more I thought about it, the more concerned I became about all the young black boys and men in that neighborhood. Did they know not to run? Did they know to stay calm and say, "It's okay"?

I began to feel embarrassed that I hadn't asserted more control during the encounter. I hadn't told the officers that what they were doing was illegal. Should I have said something? Despite the work I'd done assisting people on death row, I questioned how prepared I was to do really difficult things. I even started having second thoughts about going to Alabama to start a law office.

My complaint made it through the review process at the Atlanta Police Department. Every few weeks, I'd get a letter explaining that the police officers had done nothing wrong and that police work is very difficult. Finally, the deputy chief agreed to meet with me. I had asked for an apology and suggested training cops to avoid similar incidents. He nodded politely as I explained what had happened. When I finished, he apologized, but I suspected that he just wanted me to leave. He promised that the officers would be required to do some "extra homework on community relations." I didn't feel better.

My caseload was getting crazy. The lawyers defending the Gadsden City Jail finally admitted that Mr. Ruffin's rights had been violated and that he had been illegally denied his asthma medicine. We won a decent settlement for Mr. Ruffin's family, so they would at least receive some financial help.

By then, my death penalty docket was full. I had no time to make war with the Atlanta police when I had clients facing execution. Still, I couldn't stop thinking about how dangerous and unfair the situation was and how I'd done nothing wrong. And what if I *had* had drugs in my car? I would have been arrested—even if the police had entered the car illegally. Would I get an attorney who would take such a claim seriously? Would a judge believe that I'd done nothing wrong? Would they believe someone who was just like me but happened not to be a lawyer? Would they believe someone who was unemployed or had a prior criminal record?

I started giving talks to youth groups, churches, and community organizations about the challenges of being criminalized for being poor or a person of color and dealing with the presumption of guilt. I spoke at local meetings and argued that police could improve public safety without abusing people. That law enforcers and people in power should still be held accountable for their actions.

After one talk at a small African American church in a poor, rural county in Alabama, I was approached by an older black man in a wheelchair. He was wearing an old brown suit. I had noticed him looking at me intensely throughout my presentation. A young boy who was about twelve wheeled him over to me, probably his grandson.

"Do you know what you're doing?" the old man asked.

I tried to smile through my confusion. "I think so. . . ."

He cut me off and said loudly, "I'll tell you what you're doing. You're beating the drum for justice!" He had an impassioned look on his face. He said it again emphatically, "You've got to beat the drum for justice."

He leaned back in his chair, and I stopped smiling. Something about what he said had sobered me. I answered him softly, "Yes, sir."

He looked at me sympathetically and waved me closer. Then he spoke very quietly, almost a whisper, but with a fierceness that was unforgettable.

"You see this scar on the top of my head?" He tilted his head to show me. "I got that scar in Greene County, Alabama, trying to register to vote in 1964. You see this scar on the side of my head?" He turned his head to the left and I saw a four-inch scar just above his right ear. "I got that scar in Mississippi demanding civil rights."

His voice grew stronger. He tightened his grip on my arm and lowered his head some more. "You see that mark?" There was a dark circle at the base of his skull. "I got that bruise in Birmingham after the Children's Crusade."

He leaned back and looked at me intensely. "People think these are my scars, cuts, and bruises."

For the first time I noticed that his eyes were wet with tears. He placed his hands on his head. "These aren't my scars, cuts, and bruises. These are my medals of honor."

He stared at me for a long moment, wiped his eyes, and nodded to the boy, who wheeled him away.

I stood there with a lump in my throat, staring after him.

After a moment, I realized that the time to open the Alabama office had come.

CHAPTER THREE

Trials and Tribulation

After months of frustration, failure, and growing public scorn, Sheriff Thomas Tate, ABI lead investigator Simon Benson, and the district attorney's investigator Larry Ikner decided to arrest Walter McMillian based on Ralph Myers's allegation. They hadn't yet investigated Mr. McMillian, so they decided to arrest him on a minor pretextual charge while they built their bigger case. During Myers's strange testimonial, the suggestion that Mr. McMillian might also have sexually assaulted him arose. Alabama law had outlawed nonprocreative sex, so officials planned to arrest Mr. McMillian on those charges.

On June 7, 1987, Sheriff Tate led an army of more than a dozen officers to a backcountry road. When they found Walter's truck, they drew their weapons, forced him from his vehicle, and surrounded him. Tate told him he was under arrest. When Walter frantically asked the sheriff what he had done, the sheriff told him that he was being charged with sodomy.

Walter told the sheriff that he did not understand the meaning of the word. When the sheriff explained the charge in crude terms, Walter was incredulous and couldn't help but laugh at the notion. This provoked Tate, who unleashed a torrent of racial slurs and threats. Walter would report for years that all he heard throughout his arrest were insults and threats of lynching.

"We're going to keep all of you from running around with these white girls. I ought to take you off and hang you like we done in Mobile," Tate reportedly told Walter, referring to a haunting case in Mobile from only a few years before in which the Ku Klux Klan had lynched a young African American man named Michael Donald.

The threats of lynching terrified Walter. He was also confused. If he was being arrested for raping another man, why were they throwing questions at him about the murder of Ronda Morrison? Walter vehemently denied both allegations.

In response, the officers locked him up.

When Ted Pearson, the District Attorney of Monroe County, first heard his investigators' flimsy evidence against Walter McMillian, he must have been disappointed. Ralph Myers's story of the crime was pretty far-fetched.

Here is Myers's account of the murder of Ronda Morrison:

On the day of the murder, Myers was getting gas. Walter McMillian saw him at the gas station and forced him at gunpoint to get into Walter's truck. Myers didn't really know Walter before that day. Once in the truck, Walter told Myers he needed him to drive because Walter's arm was hurt. Myers protested but had no choice. Walter directed Myers to drive him to Jackson Cleaners in downtown Monroeville and to wait in the truck while Mr. McMillian went inside alone. After waiting a long time, Myers drove down the street to a grocery store to buy cigarettes. He returned ten minutes later. After another long wait, Mr. McMillian finally emerged from the store and returned to the truck. He immediately admitted that he had killed the store clerk. Myers then drove Mr. McMillian back to the gas station so that Myers could retrieve his vehicle. Before Myers left, Walter threatened to kill him if he ever told anyone what he had seen or done.

In summary, an African American man planning a robbery-murder in the heart of Monroeville in the middle of the day stops at a gas station and randomly selects a white man to become his accomplice by asking him to drive him to and from the crime scene because his arm is injured, even though he had been able to drive himself to the gas station where he encountered Myers and to drive his truck home after returning Myers to the gas station.

Law enforcement officers knew that Myers's story would be very difficult to prove, so they arrested Walter for sodomy, which served to shock the community and further tarnish Mr. McMillian's reputation; it also gave police an opportunity to bring Walter's truck to the jail for Bill Hooks, a jailhouse informant, to see.

Bill Hooks was a young black man with a reputation as a jailhouse snitch. He had been in the county jail on burglary charges at the time Mr. McMillian was arrested. Hooks was promised release from jail and reward money if he could connect Mr. McMillian's truck to the Morrison murder. Hooks eagerly told investigators that he had driven by Jackson Cleaners near the time of the crime and had seen a truck tear away from the cleaners with two men inside. At the jail, Hooks identified Walter's truck as the one he'd seen at the cleaners nearly six months earlier.

This second witness gave law enforcement officials what they needed to charge Walter McMillian with capital murder in the shooting death of Ronda Morrison.

There was joy and relief in the community. Finally, someone had been charged. Sheriff Tom Tate, the district attorney (DA), and other law enforcement officers were cheered.

People who knew Walter, though, found it difficult to believe he could be responsible for a sensational murder. Black residents told Sheriff Tate that he had arrested the wrong man. This was a man who had no history of crime or violence, and robbery just didn't make sense for someone who worked as hard as he did.

Tate still had not investigated Mr. McMillian himself, his life or background, or even his whereabouts on the day of the murder. He knew about the affair with Karen Kelly and had heard the rumors that Walter's independence as a black man must mean he was dealing drugs.

As it turned out, on the day of the murder, a fish fry had been held at Walter's house. Members of Walter's family spent the day out in front of the house, selling food to passersby to raise money for the local church where Evelyn Smith, Walter's sister, was a minister. There were at least a dozen church parishioners at the house all morning with Walter and his family on the day Ronda Morrison was murdered.

Walter didn't have a tree job that day. He had decided to replace the transmission in his truck and called over his mechanic friend, Jimmy Hunter, to help. By 9:30 in the morning, the two men had dismantled Walter's truck, completely removing the transmission. By 11:00, relatives had arrived and had started frying fish and other food to sell.

Police reported that the Morrison murder took place around 10:15 a.m., eleven miles or so from Mr. McMillian's home, at the same time that a dozen church members were at Walter's home selling food while Walter and Jimmy worked on his truck. In the early afternoon, Ernest Welch, a white man who worked for a local furniture store, arrived to collect money from Walter's mother for a purchase she had made on credit. Welch told the folks gathered at the house that his niece

Ronda had been murdered at Jackson Cleaners that morning. They discussed the shocking news with Welch for some time.

Dozens of people were able to confirm that Walter could not have committed the murder: church members, Walter's family, and the people who were stopping at the house to buy food. That group included a police officer who stopped by the house to buy a sandwich and noted in his police log that he had bought food at Mr. McMillian's house with Walter and a crowd of church folks present.

Based on their personal knowledge of Walter's where-abouts at the time of the Morrison murder, family members, church members, black pastors, and others all pleaded with Sheriff Tate to release Mr. McMillian. Tate wouldn't do it. The arrest had been too long in the making to admit yet another failure. He and his investigators discussed it, and agreed to stick with the accusation.

Ralph Myers was beginning to have second thoughts about accusing Mr. McMillian. He, too, was being charged in the Morrison murder. In exchange for testifying against Wal-ter, though, he'd been promised that he would be favorably treated. Now it was starting to dawn on him that admitting to involvement in a high-profile murder that he actually had nothing to do with was probably not smart.

A few days before the capital murder charges against

Mr. McMillian were made public, Myers told the police his allegations against Mr. McMillian weren't true. At this point, Tate and his investigators had little interest in Myers's denying his own story. Instead, they decided to pressure Myers to produce *more* incriminating details. When Myers protested that he didn't have more because, well, the story wasn't true, the investigators weren't having it.

Instead, on August 1, 1987, they transferred both Myers and Walter from the county jail to death row—but on separate floors so they wouldn't interact.

Death row is the most extreme punitive confinement permitted. Putting someone who has not yet had a trial into a prison reserved for convicted felons—let alone on death row—is almost never done. Even the other death row prisoners were shocked. It's unclear how Tate was able to persuade the prison warden to house two pretrial detainees on death row, although it's likely because he had connections from his days as a probation officer.

Sheriff Tate drove Walter to Holman Correctional Facility, a short ride away in Atmore, Alabama. Before the trip, the sheriff again threatened Walter with racial slurs and terrifying plans.

When Walter McMillian arrived on Alabama's death row, an entire community of condemned men awaited him. A hundred or so death row prisoners had been sentenced to execution in

Alabama since capital punishment was restored in 1975. Most of them were black, although to Walter's surprise, some were white. Everyone was poor, and everyone asked him why he was there.

Condemned prisoners on Alabama's death row unit were housed in windowless concrete buildings that were notoriously hot and uncomfortable. Each death row inmate was locked in a five-by-eight-foot cell with a metal door, a commode, and a steel bunk by themselves for twenty-three hours a day. The temperatures in August consistently reached more than 100 degrees. Incarcerated men would trap rats, poisonous spiders, and snakes they found inside the prison to pass the time and to protect themselves. Isolated and remote, most prisoners had limited opportunity for exercise or visits and were held in disturbingly close proximity to the electric chair.

The large wooden chair was built in the 1930s, and inmates had painted it yellow before attaching its leather straps and electrodes. They called it Yellow Mama. With another scheduled execution fast approaching, condemned prisoners were talking about executions constantly when Walter arrived. For his first three weeks on Alabama's death row, the horrifically botched execution of John Evans was pretty much all he heard about. Evans had been electrocuted three times over the course of fourteen minutes after electrodes were incorrectly fastened by corrections officers. The circumstances of his excruciating death haunted the other inmates.

The whirlwind of the past weeks had left Walter devastated.

His whole life he'd been unrestrained by anyone or anything; now he found himself confined in a way he could never have imagined. The racist taunts and threats from law enforcement officers who did not know him were shocking. He'd never experienced such contempt. He had always been well liked and gotten along with just about everybody. He genuinely believed the accusations against him had been a serious misunderstanding. Once officials talked to his family to confirm his alibi, he'd surely be released. When the days turned into weeks, Walter began to sink into deep despair.

His body reacted to the shock of his situation. For days, he couldn't taste anything he ate. He couldn't calm himself. When he woke each morning, he would feel normal for a few minutes and then sink into terror upon remembering where he was. Prison officials had shaved his head and all the hair from his face. Looking in a mirror, he didn't recognize himself.

He was used to working outside among the trees with the scent of fresh pine on the cool breeze. Now he found himself staring at the bleak walls of death row. Fear and anguish unlike anything he'd ever experienced settled on Walter.

The judge, Robert E. Lee Key Jr., had appointed an attorney to represent Walter for his trial. But there was something untrustworthy about this white lawyer, who didn't seem to have much interest in Walter's side of the story. Instead, his family raised money to hire the only black criminal lawyers in the region, J. L. Chestnut and Bruce Boynton from Selma. Chestnut was fiery and had done a lot of civil rights work.

Boynton's mother, Amelia Boynton Robinson, was a legendary activist; Boynton himself had strong civil rights credentials as well.

Chestnut and Boynton failed to persuade local officials to release Walter immediately. Meanwhile, Sherriff Tate was furious that Mr. McMillian had hired outside lawyers; on the trip to Holman, he mocked Walter for thinking it would make any difference. Although the money to hire Chestnut and Boynton was raised by family members through church donations and by selling their few possessions, local law enforcement pointed to it as evidence that Walter was secretly hoarding money and that he wasn't the innocent man he pretended to be.

Other prisoners had advised him to take action and file a federal complaint to fight against being illegally held on death row. When Walter, who could barely read or write, failed to file the various pleadings and lawsuits the other prisoners had advised him to file, some blamed him for his predicament.

"There were days when I couldn't breathe," Walter recalled later. "I hadn't ever experienced anything like this before in my life. I was around all these murderers, and yet it felt like sometimes they were the only ones trying to help me. I prayed, I read the Bible, and I'd be lying if I didn't tell you that I was scared, terrified just about every day."

Ralph Myers's original plan of saying he knew something about the Morrison murder had clearly backfired. He had also been charged with capital murder in the death of Ronda Morrison and sent to death row. Myers was sinking deeper into an emotional crisis. From the time he was burned as a child, he had always feared fire, heat, and small spaces. As the prisoners talked more and more about the details of executions such as John Evans's, Myers became more and more distraught.

On the night of one execution, Myers was in full crisis, sobbing in his cell. There is a tradition on death row in Alabama that, at the time scheduled for the execution, the condemned prisoners bang on their cell doors with cups in protest. At midnight, while all the other prisoners banged away, Myers curled up on the floor in the corner of his cell, hyperventilating. When the stench of burned flesh that many on the row claimed they could smell during the execution wafted into his cell, Myers dissolved. He called Tate the next morning and told him that he would say whatever he wanted if he would get him off death row.

Tate immediately picked up Myers and brought him back to the county jail. Ordinarily, the Alabama Department of Corrections couldn't just put people on death row or let them off without court orders or legal filings—and certainly no prison warden could do so on his own. But nothing about the prosecution of Walter McMillian was turning out to be ordinary.

With Myers back as the primary witness and Bill Hooks ready to say that he saw Walter's truck at the crime scene, the DA believed that he could proceed against Mr. McMillian. The case was scheduled for trial in February 1988.

The DA, Ted Pearson, was getting older and had plans to retire soon after twenty years on the job. He hated that his office had been criticized for failing to solve the Morrison murder more quickly. Pearson was determined to leave office with a victory and likely saw the prosecution of Walter McMillian as one of the most important cases of his career.

His one lingering concern may have been a recent United States Supreme Court case that threatened a long-standing feature of high-profile criminal trials in the South: the all-white jury.

Even twenty years after the civil rights revolution, Monroe County went against legal requirements of racial integration and diversity. For example, African Americans were often excluded from jury service on felony crime cases in Monroe County.

As far back as the 1880s, the Supreme Court ruled in *Strauder v. West Virginia* that excluding black people from jury service was unconstitutional, but juries remained all-white for decades afterward. In 1945, the Supreme Court upheld a Texas statute that limited the number of black jurors to exactly one per case. In Deep South states, jury rolls were pulled from voting rolls, which excluded African Americans. Even after the Voting Rights Act passed, court clerks and judges *still* kept the jury rolls mostly white through various tactics to undermine the law. Local jury commissions used statutory requirements that jurors be "intelligent and upright" to ex-clude African Americans and women.

By the 1970s, the Supreme Court ruled that under-representation of racial minorities and women in jury pools was unconstitutional. But the practice of striking all or most African American potential jurors was common. "Striking," or using peremptory strikes, is a practice that allows lawyers to reject jurors without stating a reason why. Which meant that defendants like Walter McMillian, even in counties that were 40 or 50 percent black, frequently found themselves staring at all-white juries because all the black jurors had been struck. This was especially common in death penalty cases. Then, in 1986, the Supreme Court ruled in *Batson v. Kentucky* that prosecutors could be challenged more directly about using racially discriminatory peremptory strikes. This development gave hope to black defendants—but didn't necessarily stop prosecutors from finding loopholes to continue excluding black jurors.

In cases like Walter's, which had caught the community's attention, defense lawyers will often file a motion to change venue—to move the case from the county where the crime took place to a different county where there is less publicity and eagerness to convict. Usually, though, judges reject the motion.

In October 1987, Chestnut and Boynton presented a change-of-venue motion. To their total surprise, Pearson agreed that the trial should be moved due to the amount of pretrial coverage. Judge Key nodded sympathetically. Chestnut, who knew his way around the Alabama courts, was sure something bad was about to happen. Could the judge and the DA already have a plan?

When the judge suggested that it be moved to a neighboring county so that witnesses wouldn't have far to travel, Chestnut remained hopeful. Almost all of the bordering counties had fairly large African American populations, between 32 and 72 percent black. Only wealthy Baldwin County to the south was atypical, with an African American population of just 9 percent.

The judge took very little time deciding where the trial should be moved: "We'll go to Baldwin County."

The change of venue was disastrous for Walter. Chestnut and Boynton knew there would be very few, if any, black jurors. They also understood that it was an extremely conservative county that had made even less progress than Monroe in leaving behind the racial politics of Jim Crow. Chestnut and Boynton immediately complained, but the judge reminded them it was their motion.

Walter worried about the venue change as well. But he still put his faith in this fact: no one could hear the evidence and believe that he committed this crime. He just didn't believe that a jury, black or white, could convict him on the nonsensical story told by Ralph Myers—not when he had an unquestionable alibi with close to a dozen witnesses.

Meanwhile, Ralph Myers was once again having second

thoughts. The February morning that the trial was set to begin, he told investigators that he could not testify because what they wanted him to say was not true.

The trial was postponed, and Myers was sent back to death row for refusing to cooperate. Back at Holman, it wasn't long before he again showed serious emotional and psychological distress. He was sent to the Taylor Hardin Secure Medical Facility in Tuscaloosa, the state hospital for the mentally ill. It did very little to change his predicament, though, and he was returned to death row after thirty days at the hospital. Realizing he could not escape the situation he'd created for himself, Myers finally agreed, once and for all, to testify against Walter McMillian.

A new trial date was scheduled for August 1988. By now, Walter had been on death row for over a year. As hard as he had tried to adjust, he couldn't accept the nightmare his life had become.

His lawyers seemed happy that Myers was struggling. They told Walter it was a good sign that Myers had refused to testify. But it had meant another six months on death row for Walter, and he couldn't see anything encouraging about that.

When they finally moved him to the Baldwin County Jail in Bay Minette for the August trial, Walter left death row confident he'd never return. He had befriended several men on the row and was surprised by how conflicted he felt about leaving them, knowing what they would soon face. Yet when they called his name to the transfer office, he lost no time getting in the van to leave.

The trial was short and clinical.

Jury selection lasted just a few hours. Pearson used his peremptory strikes to exclude all but one of the African Americans who had been summoned to serve on the jury. The State put Myers on the stand to tell his absurd story about Walter forcing him to drive to Jackson Cleaners. This version had Myers going into the cleaners, where he saw Walter standing over the dead body of Ronda Morrison. Bizarrely, he also claimed that a third person was present and involved in the murder, a mysterious white man with salt-and-pepper hair who was clearly in charge of the crime and who directed Walter to kill Myers, too, but Walter couldn't because he was out of bullets.

Walter thought the testimony was so nonsensical he couldn't believe that people were taking it seriously. Why wasn't everyone laughing? Chestnut's cross-examination of Myers made it clear that the witness was lying. When Chestnut finished, Walter was sure that the State would simply announce that they had made a mistake. Instead, the prosecutor brought Myers back up to repeat his accusations, as if repeating his lies enough times would make them true.

Bill Hooks testified that he'd seen Walter's truck pull out

of the cleaners at the time of the murder and that he recognized the truck because it had been modified as a "lowrider." Walter instantly whispered to his lawyers that he
hadn't turned his truck into a lowrider until several months
after Morrison was murdered. His lawyers didn't do much
with that information, which frustrated Walter. Then another
white man Walter had never heard of, Joe Hightower, took
the stand and said that he had seen the truck at the cleaners,
too.

There were a dozen people who could talk about the fish
fry and insist that Walter was at home when Ronda Morrison
was killed. His lawyers called only three of them. Everybody
seemed to be rushing to get the trial over with, and Walter
couldn't understand it. The State then called Ernest Welch,
a white man, who said he was the "furniture man" who col-
lected money at the McMillian house on the day they were
having a fish fry—but it wasn't the same day that his niece
Ronda Morrison was murdered. He said that he had been so
devastated that he went to the McMillian residence to collect
money on a different day.

The lawyers made their arguments, the jury retired, and
less than three hours later, they filed back into the courtroom.
Stone-faced, one by one, they pronounced Walter McMillian
guilty.

A week later, he sat in the van with shackles pinching his
ankles, and chains tightly wound around his waist. He could
feel his feet beginning to swell because the circulation was cut

off by the metal digging into his skin. The handcuffs were too tight, and he was becoming uncharacteristically angry.

"Why you got these chains on me this tight?"

The two Baldwin County deputies who had picked him up a week earlier had not been friendly on the ride from death row to the courthouse. Now that he had been convicted of capital murder, they were downright hostile. One seemed to laugh in response to Walter's question.

"Them chains is the same as they were when we picked you up. They just feel tighter because we got you now."

"You need to loosen this, man, I can't ride like this."

"It ain't going to happen, so you should get your mind off it."

Walter suddenly recognized the man. At the end of the trial when the jury had found Walter guilty, his family and several of the black people who had attended the trial were in shocked disbelief. Sheriff Tate claimed that Walter's twenty-four-year-old son, Johnny, said, "Somebody's going to pay for what they've done to my father." Tate asked deputies to arrest Johnny, and there was a scuffle. Walter saw the officers wrestle his child to the ground and place him in handcuffs. The more he looked at the two deputies driving him back to death row, the more convinced he became that one of them had tackled his son.

The van began to move. They wouldn't tell Walter where he was going, but as soon as they got on the road, it was clear that they were taking him back to death row.

He had been distraught and confused on the day of his arrest. He had been frustrated when the days turned into weeks at the county jail. He had been depressed and terrified when they took him to death row before he was even convicted of a crime. But when the nearly all-white jury pronounced him guilty, after fifteen months of waiting for vindication, he was shocked, paralyzed. Now he felt himself coming back to life—but all he could feel was seething anger. Walter realized that he had been foolish to give everyone—the prosecutors, the judge, the officers—the benefit of the doubt.

"Hey, I'm going to sue all of y'all!"

He knew he was screaming and that it wasn't going to make any difference. "I'm going to sue all of y'all!" he repeated. The officers paid him no attention.

"Loose these chains. Loose these chains."

He couldn't remember when he'd last lost control, but he felt himself falling apart. With some struggle he became silent.

CHAPTER FOUR

The Old Rugged Cross

In February 1989, Eva Ansley and I reached our goal of opening a new nonprofit law center in Tuscaloosa, dedicated to providing free, quality legal services to condemned men and women on death row in Alabama. We never thought it would be easy, but it turned out to be even harder than we had expected.

Obstacles were multiplying rapidly. We were denied state funding, and after several disheartening meetings with our board, it had become clear that we had no support in the state for the project. On top of that, there weren't many lawyers who would do full-time death penalty work for less than $25,000 a year in Alabama.

Eva and I realized that we would have to do it on our own and raise the money ourselves. We regrouped and started again, this time in Montgomery, the state capital. The project would eventually be named the Equal Justice Initiative (EJI).

In the summer of 1989, we signed a lease on a small

building near downtown Montgomery, a two-story Greek Revival house built in 1882, painted yellow and with a charming porch that made it feel open and welcoming. It felt like a good start—and a nice contrast from the courtrooms, waiting rooms, and prison walls that our clients' family members had to face. The office was cold in the winter, it was almost impossible to keep squirrels out of the attic, and there wasn't enough electricity to run the copier and a coffeepot at the same time without blowing a fuse. But from the start, it felt like a home and a place to work—and given the hours we would spend there, it was always a little of both.

A flood of execution dates awaited us. Between 1975, when Alabama's new death penalty statute was passed, and the end of 1988, there had been only three executions in Alabama. But by 1989, driven by shifting politics and laws, the number of people executed by the state of Alabama would double.

Months before our center opened, I started visiting Alabama's death row every month, traveling from Atlanta to see a handful of new clients, including Walter McMillian. They were all grateful for the help, but as the spring of 1989 approached, they all made the same request at the end of our meetings: Help Michael Lindsey. Lindsey's execution was scheduled for May 1989. I painfully explained how limited our time and resources were, and how frantic we were, trying to get the new EJI office up and running. Although they said they understood, they clearly felt anguished and guilty about getting legal assistance while other men faced looming executions.

Lindsey's lawyer, David Bagwell, was a respected civil attorney from Mobile. But prisoners got word of a letter Bagwell had written and talked about it among themselves, especially one chilling line: "I generally favor the death penalty because mad dogs ought to die." Many prisoners were appalled by this attitude, from someone who was supposedly an advocate for them. They became even more distrustful of lawyers, even the ones who claimed to help.

We decided to do what we could for Michael Lindsey, whose execution date was fast approaching. We tried to make arguments about an interesting twist in that case: His jury had never decided that he should be executed at all. He'd received a sentence of life imprisonment without parole from his jury, but the judge had overridden it, instead imposing a death sentence. This was unusual—and was likely because this judge was trying to appear "tough on crime" in order to get reelected.

We wrote a letter to the governor of Alabama, Guy Hunt, asking him to stop the Lindsey execution on the grounds that the jury had decided against putting him to death. Governor Hunt quickly denied our request for clemency, declaring that he would not "go against the wishes of the community expressed by the jury that Mr. Lindsey be put to death," even though we stressed that the community's representatives—the jury—had done the opposite; they clearly elected to spare Lindsey's life. It didn't matter. He was electrocuted on May 26, 1989.

· · ·

The first execution I witnessed was that of my client Herbert Richardson, a Vietnam War veteran whose brutal, nightmarish experiences left him traumatized and scarred by post-traumatic stress disorder (PTSD). One of the country's least-discussed postwar problems is how frequently combat veterans bring the traumas of war back with them and are incarcerated after returning to their communities. Herbert became one of thousands of combat veterans who end up in jail or prison after completing their military service.

I had promised Herbert I would be with him during the execution, and when I arrived at the prison, it was completely dark. Outside the prison entrance were dozens of men with guns: state troopers, local police officers, deputy sheriffs, and what appeared to be part of a National Guard unit. It was surreal to see all of these armed men gathered near midnight to make sure a life would be taken without incident.

When I got inside the visiting room, Herbert's wife and her family had less than an hour left with him to say good-bye. He was calmer than I had ever seen him. He smiled at me when I walked in and gave me a hug.

"Hey, y'all, this is my lawyer," he said, introducing me with a pride that was surprising and moving to me.

I spent the next forty-five minutes with one eye on the clock, knowing that soon, the guards would take Herbert to the back, and we would never see him alive again.

When the clock struck 10:00 p.m., the guards dragged his weeping wife and family away with great difficulty. Thirty minutes before the execution, I was brought to the cell next to the execution chamber deep inside the prison, where Herbert was being held until it was time to put him in the electric chair. They had shaved the hair off his body to facilitate a "clean" execution. The state had done nothing to modify the electric chair since the disastrous John Evans execution. I felt distraught. I had tried to read up on what should happen at an execution; I had some naively misguided hope that I could save Herbert if they did something incorrectly.

Herbert was much more emotional when he saw me than he'd been in the visitation room. It must have been humiliating to be shaved in preparation for an execution. He looked shaken and upset. When I walked into the chamber, he grabbed my hands and asked if we could pray, and we did. When we were done, his face took on a distant look and then he turned to me.

"Hey, man, thank you. I know this ain't easy for you either, but I'm grateful to you for standing with me," he said with great emotion.

I smiled and gave him a hug. His face sagged with an unbearable sadness.

"It's been a very strange day, Bryan, really strange. Most people who feel fine don't get to think all day about this being their last day alive with certainty that they will be killed. It's different than being in Vietnam . . . much stranger."

He nodded at all the officers who were milling about nervously. "It's been strange for them, too. All day long people have been asking me, 'What can I do to help you?' When I woke up this morning, they kept coming to me, 'Can we get you some breakfast?' At midday they came to me, 'Can we get you some lunch?' All day long, 'What can we do to help you?' "

Herbert sighed. "More people have asked me what they can do to help me in the last fourteen hours of my life than ever asked me in the years when I was coming up." He looked at me, and his face twisted in confusion.

I gave Herbert one last long hug. I was reflecting on all of the trauma and difficulty that had followed this well-meaning man home from Vietnam. I couldn't help but ask myself, Where were these people when he really needed them? Where were all of these helpful people when Herbert was three and his mother died? Where were they when he was seven and trying to recover from physical abuse? Where were they when he was a young teen struggling with drugs and alcohol? Where were they when he returned from Vietnam traumatized and disabled?

Herbert had made a peculiar request the week before the execution. He wanted me to get the prison to play a recording of a favorite hymn as he walked to the electric chair. Now, I watched an officer bring over a tape. The sad strains of "The Old Rugged Cross" began to play as they pulled Herbert away from me.

. . .

There was a shamefulness about the experience I couldn't shake. Everyone I saw at the prison seemed surrounded by a cloud of regret and remorse. The prison officials had pumped themselves up to carry out the execution, but even they revealed extreme discomfort and some measure of shame. Maybe I was imagining it, but it seemed everyone recognized that what was taking place was wrong. Believing in capital punishment was one thing, but the realities of systematically killing someone who is not a threat are completely different.

I couldn't stop thinking about it on the trip home. I thought about Herbert's family and about the victim's family. I thought about the visitation officer, the Department of Corrections officials, the men who were paid to shave Herbert's body so that he could be killed more efficiently. I thought about the officers who had strapped him into the chair. I kept thinking that no one could *actually* believe this was a good thing to do, or even a necessary thing to do.

The next day, there were articles in the press about the execution. Some state officials expressed happiness and excitement that an execution had taken place, but I knew that none of them had actually dealt with the details of killing Herbert. I couldn't stop thinking that we don't spend much time contemplating the details of what killing someone actually involves.

I went back to my office the next day with renewed energy. I picked up my other case files, including Walter McMillian's, and made updated plans for how to assist each client to maximize the chance of avoiding an execution.

Eventually, I recognized that all my fresh resolve didn't change much—I was really only trying to reconcile myself to the realities of Herbert's death. I was comforted by the exercise just the same. I felt more determined to recruit staff and obtain resources to meet the growing challenges of providing legal assistance to condemned people. By the end of the day, I was persuaded things would improve, even while I felt burdened by the weight of it all.

CHAPTER FIVE

Homeland

Walter's wife, Minnie Belle McMillian, and his daughter, Jackie, were waiting patiently when I pulled up to the McMillians' dilapidated house in Repton, which was off the main road leading into Monroeville.

It had been a long day. I was no longer sure what time it was. I'd spent several intense hours on death row earlier in the day with Walter going over his trial transcript. Time was critical. I should have returned to Montgomery to work on appeal pleadings, but Walter's family wanted to meet, and since they were less than an hour from the prison, I had promised to come to Monroeville.

I was surprised at the profound disrepair; this was a poor family's home. The front porch was propped on three cinder blocks; the wood flooring showed signs of rot. The blue window frames were in desperate need of paint. The yard was littered with abandoned car parts, tires, and broken pieces of furniture.

Minnie walked out the front door and apologized for the appearance of the yard as I carefully stepped onto the porch. She kindly invited me inside.

"Let me fix something for you to eat. You been at the prison all day," she said. Minnie looked tired but otherwise appeared as patient and strong as I had imagined, based on Walter's descriptions and my own guesses from our phone conversations. Because the State had made Walter's affair with Karen Kelly part of its case in court, the trial had been especially difficult for Minnie. But she looked like she was still standing strong.

"Oh, no, thank you. I appreciate it, but it's fine. Walter and I ate some things on the visitation yard."

"They don't have nothing on that prison yard but chips and sodas. Let me cook you something good."

"That's very kind, I appreciate it, but I'm really okay. I know you've been working all day, too."

"Well, yes, I'm on twelve-hour shifts at the plant. Them people don't want to hear nothing about your business, your sickness, your nerves ... and definitely nothing about your family problems." She didn't sound angry or bitter, just sad. She walked over to me, gently looped her arm with mine, and slowly led me into the house. We sat down on a sofa in the crowded living room. Chairs that didn't match were piled with papers and clothes; her grandchildren's toys were scattered on the floor.

"Work people tell you to be there, and so you got to go. I'm trying to get her through school and it ain't easy." She nodded to her daughter, Jackie, who looked back at her mother sympathetically. Jackie walked across the room and sat near us. Walter and Minnie had mentioned their children—Jackie, Johnny, and "Boot"—to me several times. Jackie's name was always followed by "She's in college." I had begun to think of her as Jackie "She's in College" McMillian. All of the kids were in their twenties but still very close and protective of their mother.

I told them about my visit with Walter and talked about the next steps in the case. They updated me on all the rumors in town currently circulating about the case.

"I believe it was that old man Miles Jackson who done it," Minnie said emphatically.

"I think it's the new owner, Rick Blair," Jackie said. "Everybody knows they found a white man's skin under that girl's fingernails where she had fought whoever killed her."

As we talked, it became clear how traumatizing the last eighteen months since Walter's arrest had been.

"The trial was the worst," Minnie said. "They just ignored what we told them about Johnny D being home. Nobody has explained to me why they did that. Why did they do that?" She looked at me as if she honestly hoped I could provide an answer.

"This trial was constructed with lies," I said. I was cautious about expressing such strong opinions to Walter's family because I hadn't investigated the case enough yet. But reading the record of his trial had outraged me—not just about the injustice done to Walter, but also about the way it had burdened the entire community. Everyone in the poor black community who talked to me about the case had expressed hopelessness.

"One lie after the other," I continued. "People were fed so many lies that by the time y'all started telling the truth, it was just easier to believe *you* were the ones who were lying. It frustrates me to even read it in the trial record, so I can only imagine how you all feel."

The phone rang, and Jackie jumped up to answer it. She came back a few minutes later. "Eddie said that people are getting restless. They want to know when he's going to be there."

Minnie stood up and straightened her dress. "Well, we should probably get going. They been waiting most of the day for you."

When I looked confused, Minnie smiled. "Oh, I told the rest of the family we would bring you down there, since it's so hard to find where they live if you've never been there before. His sisters, nephews, nieces, and other folks all want to meet you."

I followed their directions down a long, winding dirt road full of impossible turns through a heavily wooded area. We came to a short, narrow bridge with room for only one car to pass. It looked shaky and unstable, so I slowed the car to a stop.

"It's okay. It hasn't rained that much, and that's the only time when it's really a problem," Minnie said.

"What kind of problem?" I didn't want to sound scared, but we were in the middle of nowhere, and in the pitch-black night I couldn't tell whether it was a swamp, a creek, or a small river under the bridge.

"It will be all right. People drive through here every day," Jackie chimed in.

It would have been too embarrassing to turn around, so I drove slowly across the bridge and was relieved when we made it to the other side. The forest began to give way to trailers, a few small homes, and finally an entire community hidden away in the woods.

We pulled up a hill until we reached a trailer that was glowing in the darkness, lit by a fire burning in a barrel out front. Small children were playing outside; they dashed into the trailer when they saw our car pull up. As we got out of the car, a tall man greeted us. He hugged Minnie and Jackie before shaking my hand.

"They been waiting for you," he told me. "I know you probably got a lot of work to do, but we appreciate you coming to meet with us. I'm Giles, Walter's nephew."

Giles led us inside. The small home was packed with more than thirty people, whose chattering fell silent when I entered. One by one, they started to smile at me. Then, to my amazement, the room broke into loud applause. I was stunned by the gesture. No one had ever applauded me just for showing up. There were older women, younger women, men Walter's age, and several men much older. Their faces were creased with worry. When the applause had died down, I began to speak.

"Thank you, that's very kind," I started. "I'm so glad to meet you all. Mr. McMillian told me he had a large family, but I didn't expect so many of you to be here. I saw him today, and he wants me to pass along his thanks and his gratitude to all of you for sticking by him. I hope you know how much your support means. He has to wake up on death row every morning, and that's not easy. But he knows he's not alone. He talks about you all the time."

"Sit down, Mr. Stevenson," someone shouted. I took a seat on an empty couch that seemed to have been reserved for me, and Minnie sat down beside me.

"We don't have any money. We gave it all to the first lawyer," called out one of the men.

"I understand that, and I won't take a penny. I work for a nonprofit law office, and we provide legal assistance at no cost to the people we represent," I replied.

"Well, how do you pay the bills?" asked one young woman. People laughed at the question.

"We get donations from foundations and people who support our work."

An older woman spoke up. It was Armelia Hand, Walter McMillian's older sister. "We don't have much, Mr. Stevenson, but you have someone we love in your care. Anything we have, you have. These people have broken our hearts," she said.

The family shared questions and comments about Walter,

the town, race, the police, the trial, and the way the whole family was now being treated by people in the community. There seemed to be therapeutic relief in voicing their concerns to me. I began to feel encouraged that some of the information I provided maybe eased their anxiety. We started to joke some, and before I knew it, I felt embraced in a way that energized me. An older woman had given me a tall glass of sweet iced tea, and no matter how much or how little I drank, she minded my glass religiously the entire evening.

As our conversation continued, Armelia Hand again spoke up. "We were standing next to him that whole morning. . . . We *know* where he was. . . . We know what he was doing!" Her voice grew louder and more distraught. The crowd in the small trailer hummed in agreement. It was the kind of wordless testimony of struggle and anguish I heard all the time growing up in a small rural black church.

"Just about everybody in here was standing next to him, talking to him, laughing with him, eating with him. Then the police come along months later, say he killed somebody miles away at the same time we were standing next to him. Then they take him away when you know it's a lie."

She was now struggling to speak. Her hands were trembling, and the emotion in her voice was making it hard for her to get her words out.

"We were with him all day! What are we supposed to do, Mr. Stevenson? Tell us, what are we supposed to do with that?" Her face twisted in pain. "I feel like I've been convicted, too."

The small crowd responded to each statement with shouts of "Yes!" and "That's right!"

"I feel like they done put me on death row, too. What do we tell these children about how to stay out of harm's way when you can be at your own house, minding your own business, surrounded by your entire family, and they still put some murder on you that you ain't do and send you to death row?"

I sat on the crowded sofa in my suit, staring into the face of a lot of pain. I hadn't expected to have such an intense meeting when I arrived. Folks were desperate for answers and trying to reconcile themselves to a situation that made no sense. I was struggling to think of something appropriate to say, when a younger woman who was Walter's niece spoke up.

"Johnny D could have never done this no kind of way, whether we was with him or not," she said, using the nickname Walter's family and friends had given him. "He's just not like that."

By then, it was close to midnight, and it would take me at least two hours to get to Montgomery. I said my farewells and exchanged hugs with practically everyone in the room before stepping out into the dark night.

December is rarely bitter cold in South Alabama during the day, but at night the temperatures can drop, a dramatic reminder that it's winter, even in the South. Without an overcoat, I cranked up the heat for the long drive home after dropping Minnie and Jackie back at their house. The meeting with the family had been inspiring. There were clearly a lot of people who cared deeply about Walter and consequently cared about how I could help. But it was also clear that people had been traumatized by what had happened. They needed a place to share their hurt and confusion.

Walter's family and most poor black people in his community were similarly burdened by Walter's conviction. The community seemed desperate for some hope of justice. The realization left me anxious but determined.

I'd gotten used to taking calls from lots of people concerning Walter's case. Most were poor and black, and they offered encouragement and support. And occasionally, a white person for whom Walter had worked would call to offer support, like Sam Crook.

"My people were heroes of the Confederacy," Crook said. "I've inherited their land, their title, and their pride. I love this county, but I know what happened to Walter McMillian ain't right."

"Well, I appreciate your call."

"Well, I've decided I ain't going to let them string him up. I'll get some boys, and we'll go cut him down before we let them take him. I'm just not going to stand for them putting a good man down for something I know he didn't do."

Sam Crook spoke in grand proclamations. I hesitated over how to respond.

"Well . . . thank you" was all I could manage.

When I later asked Walter about Sam Crook, he just smiled. "I've done a lot of work for him. He's been good to me. He's a very interesting guy."

I saw Walter just about every other week for those first few months, and I learned some of his habits. *Interesting* was Walter's word for "odd," and having worked for hundreds of people throughout the county over the years, he'd encountered no shortage of "interesting" people. The more unusual or bizarre the person was, the more interesting they were, according to Walter. "Very interesting" and "real interesting" and finally "Now, he's reeeeaaaalll interesting" were the markers for strange and stranger characters. Walter seemed reluctant to say anything bad about anyone. He'd just chuckle if he thought someone was odd.

Walter grew much more comfortable during our visits, and sometimes he would veer into topics that had nothing to do with the case. The guards. Other prisoners. People back home who he'd thought would visit but hadn't. In these conversations, Walter showed remarkable empathy. He spent a lot of time imagining what other people were thinking and feeling. He guessed what frustrations guards must be experiencing to excuse the rude things they said to him. He gave voice to how hard it must be to visit someone on death row.

We also talked about the food he liked, jobs he'd worked when he was younger. We talked about race and power, the things we saw that were funny, and the things we saw that were sad. It made him feel better to have a normal conversation with someone who wasn't on the row or a guard, and I always spent extra time with him to talk about things unrelated to the case. Not just for him, but for myself as well. I found something refreshing in the moments I spent with clients when we didn't relate to one another as attorney and client but as friends. My work had quickly become my life, and Walter's case was becoming the most complicated and time-consuming I'd ever worked on.

"Man, all these guys talk about how you're working on their case. You must not ever get any peace," he told me once.

"Well, everybody needs help, so we're trying."

He gave me an odd look that I hadn't seen before. I think he wasn't sure whether he could give me advice—he hadn't done that yet. Finally, he looked at me earnestly and said, "Well, you know you can't help everybody. You'll kill yourself if you try to do that." He continued looking at me with concern.

I smiled. "I know."

"I mean, you gotta help *me*. You shouldn't hold nothing back on my case," he said with a smile. "I expect you to fight all comers to get me out of here. Take 'em all down, if necessary."

"Stand up to giants, slay wild beasts, wrestle alligators," I joked.

The more time I spent with Walter, the more I cared for this kind, decent man with a generous nature. He freely acknowledged that he'd made poor decisions, particularly where women were concerned. But all the friends, family, and associates who knew him agreed: Walter generally tried to do the right thing.

In all death penalty cases, spending time with clients is important. Developing the trust of clients is not only necessary to manage the complexities of the litigation and deal with the stress of a potential execution; it's also key to effective advocacy. A client's life often depends on his lawyer's ability to create a narrative that puts in context and explains his poor decisions or violent behavior. Uncovering things about someone's background that no one has previously discovered—things that might be hard to discuss but are critically important—requires trust. Getting someone to acknowledge he has been the victim of child sexual abuse, neglect, or abandonment won't happen without the kind of comfort that takes hours and multiple visits to develop. Talking about sports, TV, popular culture, or anything else the client wants to discuss is absolutely appropriate to building a relationship that makes effective work possible. But it also creates genuine connections with clients. And that's certainly what happened with Walter.

Shortly after my first trip to see Walter's family, I received a call from a young man named Darnell Houston who told me he could prove that Walter was innocent. His voice shook with nerves, but he was determined to meet with me in person. He lived in a rural part of Monroe County on farmland that his family had worked since the time of slavery.

When I arrived at his home, he walked out to greet me. He was a young black man in his twenties with a worried demeanor. As soon as we sat down, he got right to business.

"Mr. Stevenson," he began. "I can prove that Walter McMillian is innocent."

"Really?"

"Bill Hooks is lying. I found out that he testified that he drove by that cleaners on the day that girl was killed, and that's a lie."

"How do you know?"

"We were working together all that day. We both worked at the NAPA auto parts store last November. I remember that Saturday when that girl was killed because ambulances and police started racing up the street."

"You were working on the Saturday morning that Ronda Morrison was killed?"

"Yes, sir, with Bill Hooks, from about eight in the morning till we closed after lunch, *after* all them ambulances went by our shop. It was probably close to eleven when the sirens started. Bill was working on a car in the shop with me. There ain't but one way out the store; he never left the entire morning. If he said he drove by the cleaners when that girl was killed, he's lying."

One of the most frustrating things about reading Walter's trial record had been that the State's witnesses—Ralph Myers, Bill Hooks, and Joe Hightower—were so obviously not believable. Their testimony was laughably inconsistent and completely lacking in credibility. Myers's account of his role in the crime—Walter kidnapping him to drive him to the crime scene and then dropping him off afterward—never made any sense. Hooks's response to every line of questioning was to repeat over and over again that he saw Walter McMillian walk out of the store with a bag, get into his lowrider truck, and get driven away by a white man. He could not answer any questions about what else he saw that day or what he was doing in the area.

My plan had been to immediately challenge Walter's conviction to the Alabama Court of Criminal Appeals. The State had done so little to prove Walter's guilt that there weren't a lot of legal issues to appeal, but the evidence against him was so unpersuasive that I was hopeful the court might overturn the conviction simply because it was so unreliable. Once the case was on direct appeal, no new evidence would be considered. The timing for filing a motion for a new trial in the trial court—the last chance to introduce new facts before an appeal begins—had already expired. Chestnut and Boynton, Walter's lawyers for the initial trial, had filed a motion before withdrawing, and Judge Key had quickly denied it. Darnell said he'd told Walter's former lawyers what he told me and they had raised it in the motion for a new trial, but no one took it seriously.

In capital cases, a motion for a new trial is rarely granted. But if the defendant claims new evidence that could lead to a different outcome in the case—or that undermines the reliability of the trial—there is typically a hearing. After speaking with Darnell, I thought about refiling his assertions before the case went up on appeal. Maybe, just maybe, we could persuade local officials to retreat from the case against Walter. I made a motion to reconsider the denial of a new trial for Walter. I got an affidavit (official statement) from Darnell stating that Hooks's testimony was a lie. I took the risk of talking to a few local lawyers about whether the new prosecutor might acknowledge that the conviction was unreliable and support a new trial if there was compelling new evidence.

I was still sorting out how to proceed when Darnell called me at my office.

"Mr. Stevenson, you have to help. They arrested me this morning and took me to the jail. I just got out on bond."

"What?"

"I asked them what I had done." He sounded terrified. "They just came and arrested me and told me I had been indicted for perjury."

"Perjury? Based on what you told Mr. McMillian's lawyers a year ago?"

I hung up with Darnell, shocked and furious. Indicting someone for perjury, or lying under oath, without any investigation or evidence was unheard of. Police and prosecutors had found out that Darnell was talking to us and they decided to punish him for it. Indicting Darnell was a worrisome signal that the prosecutors were willing to threaten and intimidate people who contradicted them.

. . .

I called Tom Chapman, Monroe County's new district attorney, to set up a meeting to discuss why authorities had arrested Darnell for speaking up. I'd heard that Chapman, a former criminal defense attorney, would be fairer and more sympathetic to someone wrongly convicted than lifelong prosecutor Ted Pearson. Chapman was in his forties and had talked about modernizing law enforcement in the region. I was hopeful.

On my way to his office, I decided to give him a chance to explain what was going on. This was my first meeting with anyone associated with Walter's prosecution, and I didn't want to begin with an angry accusation. Perhaps the people who had prosecuted Walter were just misguided, even incompetent. I knew some of them were bigoted and abusive, but I guess I held out the hope that they could be reoriented.

The Monroe County courthouse is situated in the heart of downtown Monroeville. I walked through it until I found the DA's office. I announced myself to the secretary, who eyed me suspiciously before directing me into Chapman's office.

I'd met prosecutors who dressed like they would rather be out hunting ducks than running a law office, but Chapman was professional and courteous, and approached me with a pleasant demeanor. I was intrigued and looked forward to a candid conversation. After we chatted for a bit, I got down to business.

"I'm very concerned about this McMillian case. I've read

the record, and to be honest, I have serious doubts about his guilt and the reliability of this conviction."

"Well, this was a big case, there's no doubt about that. You do understand that I didn't have anything to do with the prosecution, don't you?" he replied.

"Yes, I do." I nodded.

"This was one of the most outrageous crimes in Monroe County history, and your client made a lot of people here extremely angry. People are still angry, Mr. Stevenson. There's not enough bad that can happen to Walter McMillian for some of them."

This was a disappointing beginning—he seemed completely convinced of Walter's guilt. But I pressed on.

"Well, it was an outrageous, tragic crime, so anger is understandable," I said. "But it doesn't accomplish anything to convict the wrong person. Whether Mr. McMillian has done anything wrong is what the trial should resolve. If the trial is unfair, or if witnesses have given false testimony, then we can't really know whether he's guilty or not."

"Well, you may be the only person right now who thinks the trial was unfair. Like I said, I wasn't involved in the prosecution."

I was becoming frustrated, and Chapman probably saw me shift in my seat. I thought about the dozens of black people I'd met who had complained bitterly about Walter's prosecution, and I was starting to see Chapman as either naive or willfully indifferent—or worse.

"I'm not the only person with questions about this case, Mr. Chapman. There's a whole community of people, some of whom claim to have been with Walter McMillian miles away when the crime was committed, who believe in his innocence. There are people for whom he's worked who are absolutely convinced that he did not commit this crime."

"I've talked to some of those people," Chapman responded, "and they can only have uninformed opinions. They don't have facts. Look, I can tell you right now that nobody cares who slept with Karen Kelly. There is evidence that implicates Walter McMillian for this murder, and my job is to defend this conviction." He was becoming more argumentative, and his previously calm voice was rising in anger.

"Do you intend to prosecute everyone who challenges the evidence?" My voice was now rising in exactly the way I wanted to avoid, but I was provoked by his attitude. "A perjury indictment seems like a tactic designed to intimidate and discourage people from coming forward with evidence that contradicts the State's case. The charge against Mr. Houston seems really inappropriate, Mr. Chapman, and legally indefensible."

I knew I was lecturing him, but I wanted him to know that we were going to defend Walter in a serious way.

Chapman's voice shifted from argumentative to blandly matter-of-fact. "Don't worry, I may drop the perjury charges against Houston. Now that the judge has denied your motion to reopen the case, I don't have any interest in pursuing charges against Darnell Houston. But I do want people to know that if they make false statements concerning this case, they are going to be held accountable."

I was confused and a little stunned.

"What are you talking about? The motion to reconsider has been denied?"

"Yes, the judge has already denied your motion. You must not have gotten your copy of his order. He's down in Mobile now, so sometimes there are mail issues."

I tried to conceal my surprise about the court's ruling on the motion without even permitting a hearing. I asked, "So you have no interest in investigating what Darnell Houston is saying about the possibility that the State's main witness may be lying?"

"Ralph Myers is the State's main witness."

It was clear that Chapman had looked more deeply into the case than he had initially claimed.

"Without Hooks's testimony, the conviction wouldn't be valid," I said, leveling my voice. "State law requires confirmation of accomplice testimony, which can only come from Hooks. Mr. Houston says that Hooks is lying, which makes his testimony a critical issue that should be heard in court."

I knew I was right. I knew that what I was saying wouldn't persuade Chapman, but I felt the need to say it anyway.

I left his office extremely frustrated. Reading the record had shown me that there were people who were willing to ignore evidence, logic, and common sense. Their only goal was to convict someone and reassure the community that the crime had been solved and the murderer punished.

I'd seen the abuse of power in many cases before, but there was something especially upsetting about it here, where not only a single defendant was being victimized but an entire community as well. I filed my stack of motions in Darnell's case just to make sure that they knew we would fight them.

Darnell was thrilled to hear that the charges against him would be dropped, but he was still shaken by the whole experience.

"Mr. Stevenson, all I wanted to do is tell the truth. I can't go to jail, and I'll be honest—these folks have scared me."

"I understand," I said, "but what they did is illegal and I want you to know you have done nothing wrong. They're the ones who have acted very, very inappropriately. They're trying to intimidate you." I reminded him that I was now his lawyer, and that he could refer anyone who gave him trouble to me. He looked a little relieved but was still pretty rattled when I left.

I got in my car with the sinking realization that if everyone who tried to help us on this case was going to be threatened, it would be very difficult to prove Walter's innocence. Arresting someone for coming forward with credible evidence that challenged the reliability of a capital murder conviction? The more I thought about it, the more disoriented and provoked I became. It was also sobering. If they arrested people who said things that were inconvenient, how would they react if I challenged them even harder?

CHAPTER SIX

Surely Doomed

"He's just a little boy." It was late, and I had picked up the phone after hours because no one else was in the building; it was becoming a bad habit. The older woman on the other end of the line was pleading with me after offering a heartfelt description of her grandson, who had just been jailed for murder.

"He's already been in the jail for two nights, and I can't get to him. I'm in Virginia, and my health is not good. Please tell me you'll do something."

I hesitated before answering her. Only a handful of countries permitted the death penalty for children—and the United States was one of them. Many of my Alabama clients were on death row for crimes they were accused of committing when they were sixteen- or seventeen-year-old children. Many states had changed their laws to make it easier to prosecute children as adults, and my clients were getting younger and younger.

Alabama had more juveniles sentenced to death per capita than any other state—or any other country in the world. I was determined to manage the growing demand for our services by taking on new cases only if the client was facing execution or formally condemned to death row.

I heard her murmuring on the other end, and realized she was praying. I waited until she was finished before saying, "Ma'am, I can't take the case, but I will drive down to the jail and see your grandson tomorrow. I'll see what I can do. We likely won't be able to represent him, but let me find out what's going on, and perhaps we can help you find a lawyer who can assist you."

"Mr. Stevenson, I'm so grateful."

I was tired and already feeling overwhelmed with the number of cases I had. But I needed to go to a courthouse near the county where this boy was being held, so it wouldn't be that big a deal to stop by and see the boy.

The next morning, I drove for over an hour to the county. When I got to the courthouse, I checked the clerk's file on the case and read the boy's case file, which mostly confirmed everything the grandmother had told me.

Charlie was fourteen years old. He weighed less than a hundred pounds and was just five feet tall. He didn't have any juvenile criminal history—no prior arrests, no misconduct in school, no delinquencies or prior court appearances. He was a good student who had earned several certificates for perfect attendance at his school. His mother described him as a "great kid" who was well-behaved. But Charlie had, by his own account, shot and killed a man named George.

George was Charlie's mother's boyfriend. She referred to their relationship as a "mistake." George would often come home drunk and begin acting violently. There were three occasions in the year and a half leading up to the night of the shooting when George beat Charlie's mother so mercilessly that she required medical treatment. She never left George or made him leave.

On the night of the shooting, Charlie and his mother were playing cards when George came home very drunk. "Hey, where are you?" he shouted when he came in. The two adults had argued earlier in the evening because she had begged him not to go out, fearing that he would come home drunk. Now she looked at him angrily when she saw him standing there, reeking of alcohol. He looked back at her with contempt, and in a flash, he punched her hard in the face. She didn't expect him to hit her so quickly or violently—he hadn't done it like that before. She collapsed to the floor.

Charlie was standing behind his mother and saw her head slam against their metal kitchen counter as she fell. George saw Charlie standing there and glared at him coldly before brushing past him toward the bedroom, where Charlie heard him fall noisily onto the bed. Charlie's mother was lying on the floor, unconscious and bleeding badly. He knelt by his mother's side, trying feverishly to revive her. He started crying, futilely asking his mother what to do. He frantically searched for the cloth kitchen towel because he thought it would stop the bleeding. He found it wrapped around a pot on the stove. His mother had cooked black-eyed peas for dinner; he loved black-eyed peas. They'd eaten together before they started playing pinochle, his favorite card game.

Charlie was quietly begging his mother to wake up, when it appeared to him that she wasn't breathing. He thought he should call an ambulance, but the phone was in the bedroom with George. George had never hit Charlie, but he terrified him just the same.

The house was quiet. The only sound he heard was George breathing heavily in the other room; soon he could hear him snoring.

His mother hadn't moved in nearly fifteen minutes. Charlie thought his mother might be dying or was maybe even already dead. He had to call an ambulance. He stood up, flooded with anxiety, and cautiously made his way to the bedroom. Charlie saw George on the bed asleep and felt a surge of hatred for this man. He had never liked him, never understood why his mother had let him live with them. George didn't like Charlie, either; he was rarely friendly to the boy. His mother had told Charlie that George could be sweet, but Charlie never saw any of that. Charlie knew that George's first wife and child had been killed in a car accident, and Charlie's mom said that was why he drank so much. In the eighteen months that George lived with them, it seemed to Charlie that there had been nothing but violence, loud arguments, pushing and shoving, threats, and turmoil. His mother had stopped smiling the way she used to; she'd become nervous and jumpy, *And now,* he thought, *she's on the kitchen floor, dead.*

Charlie walked to the dresser against the back wall of the bedroom to reach the phone. When he reached the phone, he wasn't sure why he didn't just pick up the receiver. He could never really explain why he opened the dresser drawer instead, put his hand under the folded white T-shirts his mom had laundered, and felt for the handgun he knew George kept hidden there. He'd never fired a gun before, but he knew he could do it.

Charlie walked over to the bed, his arms stretched out, pointing the gun at George's head. As Charlie hovered over him, the snoring stopped. The room grew very, very quiet. And that's when Charlie pulled the trigger.

The sound of the bullet firing was much louder than Charlie had expected. The gun jerked and pushed Charlie a step back; he almost lost his balance and fell. He looked at George and squeezed his eyes closed; it was horrible. He could feel himself starting to tremble again, and that's when he heard his mother moaning in the kitchen. He couldn't believe she was alive. He ran back to the phone and called 911, then sat next to her until the police arrived.

. . .

After learning all of this, I felt that no court would not prosecute Charlie as an adult. According to the file and the notes from the initial court appearance, the prosecutor did not dispute Charlie and his mother's account. It was only when I continued reading that I discovered that George was a local police officer. "George was a law enforcement officer who served with honor," the prosecutor argued. "It is a great loss for the county and a tragedy that a good person could be so heartlessly killed by this young man." The prosecutor insisted that Charlie be tried as an adult, and he announced that he intended to seek the maximum punishment permitted by law. The judge agreed. Charlie was immediately taken to the county jail for adults.

The small county jail was across the street from the courthouse. I stepped outside and walked to the jail to see this young man. The jailers clearly didn't receive a lot of out-of-town lawyers for legal visits. The deputy on duty looked at me suspiciously before taking me inside, where I waited in the small attorney meeting room. From the time I finished reading the file, I couldn't stop thinking about how tragic this case was—and my somber thoughts weren't interrupted until a small child was pushed into the visiting room. This boy seemed way too small, way too thin, and way too scared to be fourteen. I looked at the jailer, who seemed to share my surprise at how small and terrified the child appeared. I asked him to remove the handcuffs. He removed Charlie's handcuffs before leaving the room.

Charlie sat down across from me at a table. It had been three days since his arrest.

"Charlie, my name is Bryan. Your grandmother called me and asked me if I would come and see you. I'm a lawyer, and I help people who get in trouble or who are accused of crimes, and I'd like to help you."

The boy wouldn't make eye contact with me. He was tiny, but he had big, beautiful eyes. He had a close haircut that made him look even younger than he was. I thought I saw tattoos or symbols on his neck, but when I looked more closely, I realized that they were bruises.

"Charlie, are you okay?"

He was staring intensely to my left, looking at the wall as if he saw something there. His distant look was so alarming that I actually turned to see if there was something of interest behind me, but it was just a blank wall. I sat and waited for a very long time in the hope that he would give me some kind of response, but the room remained silent. He stared at the wall and then looked down at his own wrists, rubbing the spot where the metal had pinched him.

"Charlie, I want to make sure you're doing okay, so I just need you to answer a few questions for me, okay?" I knew he could hear me; whenever I spoke, he would lift his head and return his gaze to the spot on the wall.

"Charlie, if I were you, I'd be pretty scared and really

worried right now, but I'd also want someone to help me. I'd like to help, okay?" I waited for a response, but none was forthcoming.

"Charlie, can you speak? Are you okay?" He didn't say a word.

"We don't have to talk about George. We don't have to talk about what happened; we can talk about whatever you want. Is there something you want to talk about?" I was waiting for longer and longer stretches after each question, desperately hoping that he would say something, but he didn't.

"Do you want to talk about your mom? She's going to be fine. I've checked, and even though she can't visit you, she's going to be fine. She's worried about you."

I thought talking about his mother would spark something in Charlie's eyes. When it didn't, I became even more concerned about the child.

I sat down beside him and spoke more softly, "Charlie, you've got to talk to me. I can't help you if you don't. Would you just say your name—say something, please?" He continued to stare at the wall. I sat in the chair next to him, leaned close, and said quietly, "Charlie, I'm really sorry if you're upset, but please talk to me. I can't help you if you don't talk to me." He leaned back in his chair for the first time, nearly placing his head on the wall behind us. I pulled my chair closer to him and leaned back in mine. We sat silently for a long time and then I started saying silly things, because I didn't know what else to do.

"Well, you won't tell me what you're thinking, so I guess I'm going to just have to tell you what I'm thinking. I bet you think you know what I'm thinking," I said playfully, "but in fact you really couldn't possibly imagine. You probably think I'm thinking about the law, or the judge, or the police, or why won't this young man speak with me. But what I'm actually thinking about is food. Yes, that's right, Charlie," I continued teasingly, "I'm thinking about fried chicken and collard greens cooked with turkey meat and sweet potato biscuits. . . . You ever had a sweet potato biscuit?"

Still nothing. I kept going.

"I'm thinking about getting a new car because my car is so old."

I waited. Nothing.

"Charlie, you're supposed to say, 'How old is it, Bryan?' and then I say my car is so old—"

He never smiled or responded; he just continued looking at the spot on the wall, his face frozen in sadness.

After a while I tried again. "Come on, Charlie, what's going on? You've got to talk to me, son." I started leaning on him somewhat playfully, until he sat forward a bit, and then I finally felt him lean back into me. I took a chance and put my arm around him, and he immediately began to shake. His trembling intensified before he finally leaned completely into me and started crying. I put my head to his and said, "It's okay, it's all right." He was sobbing when he finally spoke. It didn't take me long to realize that he wasn't talking about what had happened with George or with his mom but about what had happened at the jail.

"There were three men who hurt me on the first night. They touched me and made me do things." Tears were streaming down his face. His voice was high-pitched and strained with anguish.

"They came back the next night and hurt me a lot," he said, becoming more hysterical with each word. Then he looked in my face for the first time.

"There were so many last night. I don't know how many there were, but they hurt me. . . ."

He was crying too hard to finish his sentence. He gripped my jacket with a force I wouldn't have imagined he was capable of exerting.

I held him and told him as gently as I could, "It's going to be okay. It's going to be okay." I'd never held anyone who gripped me as tightly as that child or who cried as hard or as long. It seemed like his tears would never end. I promised him that I would try to get him out of there right away. He begged me not to leave, but I assured him that I would be back that day. We never talked about the crime.

When I left the jail, I was more angry than sad. I kept asking myself, "Who is responsible for this? How could we ever allow this?" I went directly to the sheriff's office and explained to the sheriff what the child had told me. The sheriff listened with a distracted look on his face, but when I said I was going to see the judge, he agreed to move the child into a protected area immediately. When I told the judge and prosecutor that the child had been sexually abused and raped, they agreed to move him to a nearby juvenile facility within the next several hours.

I decided to take on the case. We ultimately got Charlie's case transferred to juvenile court, where the shooting was adjudicated as a juvenile offense. That meant Charlie wouldn't be sent to an adult prison, and he would likely be released before he turned eighteen, in just a few years. I visited Charlie regularly, and in time he recovered. He was a smart, sensitive child who was tormented by what he'd done and what he'd been through.

At a talk I gave at a church months later, I spoke about Charlie and the plight of incarcerated children. Afterward, an older married couple approached me and insisted that they had to help Charlie. I tried to dissuade these kind people from thinking they could do anything, but I gave them my card and told them they could call me. I didn't expect to hear from them, but within days they called, and they were persistent. We eventually agreed that they would write a letter to Charlie and send it to me to pass on to him. When I received the letter weeks later, I read it. It was remarkable.

Mr. and Mrs. Jennings were a white couple in their mid-seventies from a small community northeast of Birmingham. They were kind and generous people who were active in their local United Methodist church. They spoke softly and always seemed to be smiling but never appeared to be anything less than completely genuine and compassionate. They dressed like farmers and owned ten acres of land, where they grew vegetables and lived simply. Their one and only grandchild, whom they had helped raise, had committed suicide when he was a teenager, and they had never stopped grieving for him. Their grandson struggled with mental health problems during his short life, but he was a smart kid and they had been putting money away to send him to college. They explained in their letter that they wanted to use the money they'd saved for their grandson to help Charlie.

Eventually, Charlie and this couple began corresponding, building up to the day when the Jenningses met Charlie at the juvenile detention facility. They later told me that they "loved him instantly." Charlie's grandmother had died a few months after she first called me, and his mother was still struggling after the tragedy of the shooting and Charlie's incarceration. Charlie had been apprehensive about meeting with the Jenningses because he thought they wouldn't like him, but he told me after they left how comforting and caring they were. The couple became his family.

At one point early on, I tried to caution them against expecting too much from Charlie after his release. "You know, he's been through a lot. I'm not sure he can just carry on as if nothing has ever happened. I want you to understand he may not be able to do everything you'd like him to do."

They never accepted my warnings. Mrs. Jennings told me, "I know that some have been through more than others. But if we don't expect more from each other, hope better for one another, and recover from the hurt we experience, we are surely doomed."

The Jenningses helped Charlie get his general equivalency degree in detention and insisted on financing his college education. They were there, along with his mother, to take him home when he was released.

CHAPTER SEVEN

Justice Denied

I'd filed a lengthy brief about the McMillian case to the Alabama Court of Criminal Appeals, documenting the following:

Lack of evidence

Unreliable testimonies

Prosecutorial misconduct

Racially discriminatory jury selection

An improper change of venue

I even challenged Judge Robert E. Lee Key Jr.'s override of the jury's life sentence—though really, reducing an innocent man's death sentence to life imprisonment would *still* have been a failure of justice.

Walter's appeal was denied. The court rejected all of my arguments, affirming his conviction and death sentence in a seventy-page opinion. It was devastating.

I didn't think it would turn out this way. At the oral argument months earlier, I'd been hopeful as I walked into the imposing Alabama Judicial Building and stood in the grand appellate courtroom. It stood across the street from the historic Dexter Avenue Baptist Church, where Dr. Martin Luther King Jr. had pastored during the Montgomery bus boycott. It was also a block away from the state capitol, which was adorned with the battle flag of the Confederacy.

The chief judge of the court was former governor John Patterson, who had made national news in the 1960s as a fierce opponent of civil rights and racial integration with the backing of the Ku Klux Klan. When he was attorney general before becoming governor, Patterson banned the National Association for the Advancement of Colored People (NAACP) from operating in Alabama and blocked civil rights boycotts and protests. As governor, he withheld law enforcement protection for the Freedom Riders—the black and white college students and activists who traveled south in the early 1960s to desegregate public facilities in recognition of new federal laws. When the Freedom Riders' bus traveled through Alabama, they were abandoned by the police. Alone and unprotected, they were beaten violently, and their bus was bombed.

In spite of that history, I forced myself to be hopeful. That was all long ago. During my argument, the court's five judges looked at me with curiosity but asked few questions. I chose to interpret their silence as agreement.

. . .

I drove to the prison to deliver the update. Walter didn't say anything as I explained the situation, but he had a despairing look on his face. I had tried to prepare him for the possibility that it could take years to get his conviction overturned, but he had gotten his hopes up.

"They aren't ever going to admit they made a mistake," he said glumly. "They know I didn't do this. They just can't admit to being wrong, to looking bad."

"We're just getting started, Walter," I told him. "They don't know what we now know about your innocence. As soon as we present the new evidence to them, they'll think differently."

My hopefulness was genuine, in spite of everything that had happened already. For one thing, after filing the appeal brief, I had continued investigating the case intensively. I'd finally been able to hire some additional lawyers for EJI, which gave me more time to uncover even more evidence of Walter's innocence.

One new hire was Michael O'Connor, whose passion for helping people in trouble had been kindled by his own struggles with drug addiction earlier in life. The son of Irish immigrants, Michael had grown up outside of Philadelphia in a tough working-class neighborhood. Throughout his struggle overcoming addiction, his family had never abandoned him. His academic credentials got him into Yale Law School, but his heart was still connected to all the brokenness his years on the street had shown him. He was a perfect hire for EJI.

Without hesitation, he jumped into the McMillian case with me. We spent days tracking leads, interviewing dozens of people, following wild rumors, investigating different theories. Michael's help was vital, and I was grateful finally to have someone around to share the insanity of the case with—just as I was discovering that it was even crazier than I thought.

After a few months of investigation, we discovered that not only had Bill Hooks been lying, he had been paid $5,000 by Sheriff Tate to testify against Walter. We also found out that Hooks had been released from jail immediately after giving the police his statement that he'd seen Walter's lowrider truck at the cleaners on the day of the murder. Court records revealed that the DA and the sheriff, who are *county* officials, had somehow gotten *city* charges and fines against Hooks dismissed, even though they had no authority in city courts. Under US Supreme Court precedent, the State was legally obligated to reveal *all* of this to Walter's counsel before the trial.

But, of course, they hadn't.

We also found the white man who was running the store on the day that Ralph Myers came in for the purpose of giving a note to Walter. The store owner recounted his memory of that day: Myers had to ask the store owner which of the several black men in the store was Walter McMillian. The store owner was adamant that Myers had never seen Walter McMillian before.

In a church basement, Walter's sister found flyers advertising the fish fry held at Walter's house; they confirmed that the event had taken place on the same day as the Morrison murder. We even tracked down Clay Kast, the white mechanic who had modified Walter's truck and converted it to a lowrider. He confirmed that the work had been done more than six months *after* Ronda Morrison was murdered. This proved that Walter McMillian's truck had had no modifications or special features and therefore could not have been the truck described by Myers and Hooks at the trial.

I was feeling very good about the progress we were making, when I got a call that would become the most significant break in the case.

The voice said, "Mr. Stevenson, this is Ralph Myers."

Before I could compose myself, he spoke again.

"I think you need to come and see me. I have something I need to tell you."

Michael and I had started running a few miles at night after work to help us wind down from the increasingly long workdays. That evening we spent our run discussing Myers.

"Why would Myers call us now?" Michael asked. "Can you imagine just going into a courtroom and straight-up making up a story that puts an innocent man on death row? I'm not sure we can trust anything he says."

"Well, you may be right," I replied, "but he had a lot of help in putting together that testimony. Remember, they also put Myers on death row to coerce some of those statements. Who knows? He may be in touch with the State now, and this is some kind of setup where they are trying to mislead us."

I hadn't seriously considered that possibility until our run that night. I thought again about how sleazy Myers had been during the trial. We agreed that depending on what he had to say, Myers could change everything for us. His bizarre accusations and testimony were the core of the State's entire case.

Having read Myers's testimony and reviewed the records that were available about him, I knew that he had a tragic background and a complex personality. Walter and his family had described Myers as pure evil for the lies he had told during the trial. The experience of being so coldly lied about at trial by someone you don't even know was one of the most disturbing parts of the trial for Walter. I told him we'd heard from Myers and that we would see what he had to say. Walter warned me: "He's a snake. Be careful."

Three days later, Michael and I drove two hours to the maximum-security state prison in Springville, where Myers was imprisoned. We were admitted through secure metal doors into the large visitation area. There were vending machines along the wall and small rectangular tables where inmates could meet with family members. Michael and I put down our notepads and pens and paced around the room, waiting.

When Myers walked in, I was surprised at how old he seemed. His hair was gray, which made him seem frail and vulnerable. He was also shorter than I was expecting. His testimony had caused so much anguish for Walter and his family that I had created a larger-than-life image of him. He walked toward us but stopped short when he saw Michael and nervously blurted out, "Who is he? You didn't tell me you were bringing anybody with you." Myers had a thick Southern accent. Up close, his scars made him appear more sympathetic than menacing or villainous.

"This is Michael O'Connor. He's a lawyer in my office, working with me on this case."

"Well, people told me I could trust you. I don't know anything about him."

"I promise, he's fine." I glanced over at Michael, who was trying his best to look trustworthy. "Please have a seat."

He looked at Michael skeptically and then slowly sat down. My plan was to try to ease him into the conversation by letting him know that we just wanted the truth. But before I could say anything, Myers blurted out, "I lied. Everything I said at McMillian's trial was a lie. I've lost a lot of sleep and have been in a lot of pain over this. I can't be quiet any longer."

"The testimony you gave at trial against Walter McMillian was a lie?" I asked cautiously.

My heart was pounding, but I tried to stay as steady as I could. I was afraid that if I seemed too eager or too surprised— too *anything*—he might retreat.

"It was all a lie. What I'm going to tell you is going to blow your mind, Mr. Stevenson."

"Mr. Myers, you know I'm going to want you to not only tell me the truth but also tell the court the truth. Are you willing to do that?"

I was nervous to push so quickly, but I needed to be clear. I didn't want a private performance.

"That's why I called you." He sounded surprised that there could be any question about his intentions. "I've been in a group therapy class here. You're supposed to be real honest. We been talking about honesty for nearly three months. Last week, people were talking about all the bad crap that happened to them when they were kids and all the bad things they done."

Myers was picking up steam as he spoke.

"I finally told the group, 'Well, I can top all you, I done put a damn man on death row by lying in damn court.'"

He paused dramatically.

"After I told all of 'em what I'd done, everybody said I needed to make it right. That's what I'm tryin' to do." He paused again to let me take it all in. "Hey, y'all gonna buy me a soda, or am I just gonna sit here all day looking at them vending machines and pouring my heart out?" He smiled for the first time since we'd been together. Michael jumped up and walked over to buy him a drink.

"Sunkist Orange, if they got it."

For more than two hours, Ralph answered our questions. By the end, he did, in fact, blow my mind.

He told us that the sheriff and the ABI had threatened him with the death penalty if he didn't testify against Walter McMillian.

He made accusations of official corruption, talked about his involvement in the Vickie Pittman murder, and revealed his earlier attempts to recant (retract) his testimony about Walter.

He ultimately admitted that he had never known *anything* about the Ronda Morrison murder, had no clue what had happened to her or anything else at all about the crime.

He said that he had told lots of people—from the DA on down—that he had been coerced to testify falsely against Walter.

If even half of what he said was true, there were a lot of people involved in this case who knew, straight from the mouth of his accuser, that Walter McMillian had had nothing to do with the murder of Ronda Morrison.

Ralph was on his third Sunkist Orange when he stopped his stream of confessions, leaned forward, and beckoned us closer. He spoke in a whisper to Michael and me.

"You know they'll try to kill you if you actually get to the bottom of everything."

We would learn that Ralph could never let a meeting end without dropping some final dramatic insight, observation, or prediction. I reassured him that we would be careful.

. . .

On the drive back to Montgomery, Michael and I debated how much we could trust Myers. His story at trial was so ridiculous that it was easy to believe that he had been pressured to lie. But the corruption he had just exposed was harder to assess. Myers now claimed to have committed the Vickie Pittman murder under the direction of another local sheriff; he laid out to us a widespread conspiracy involving police, drug dealing, and money laundering. It was quite a tale.

We spent weeks following up on the leads that Myers had provided. He admitted to us that he had never met Walter and only knew of him through Karen Kelly. So we decided to confirm the story with Kelly herself, now a prisoner at the Tutwiler Prison for Women, where she was serving a ten-year sentence for the Pittman murder. We were told to wait for Karen Kelly in a very small room that was empty except for a square table.

Kelly was a slender white woman in her mid-thirties who walked into the room wearing no restraints or handcuffs. She seemed surprisingly comfortable, shaking my hand confidently before nodding at Michael. She sat down and announced that Walter had been framed and that she was grateful finally to be able to tell someone. When we began with our questions, she quickly confirmed that Myers had not known Walter before the Morrison murder.

"Ralph is a fool. He thought he could trust those crooked cops, and he let them talk him into saying he was involved with a crime he didn't know anything about. He's done enough bad that he didn't need to go around making stuff up."

Though she was calm at the outset of our interview, she became increasingly emotional as she started detailing the events surrounding the case. She wept more than once. She spoke with remorse about how her life had spiraled out of control when she started abusing drugs. She was especially upset that Walter was on death row.

"I feel like I'm the reason that he's in prison. He's just not the kind of person that would kill somebody, I know that." Then her tone turned bitter. "I made a lot of mistakes, but those people should be ashamed. They've done just as much bad as I've done. Sheriff Tate only had one thing on his mind. He just kept saying, 'Why you want to sleep with one of them?' It was awful, and he's awful." She paused and looked down at her hands. "But I'm awful, too. Look at what I've done," she said sadly.

Michael and I decided to spend more time looking into the murder of Vickie Pittman. We hoped that by understanding the Pittman case, and documenting the other false things Myers had asserted about it, we could further disprove the reliability of the Morrison trial.

Vickie Pittman's murder had been all but forgotten. Monroe County officials had reduced Myers's and Kelly's sentences in exchange for Myers's testimony against Walter. How they managed to reduce sentences in the Pittman case, which was outside their jurisdiction in another county, was another mystery. Myers insisted that there were other people besides him and Kelly involved in the Pittman murder, including a corrupt local sheriff. Myers told us that she was murdered for threats she had made to expose corruption.

We had learned from some of the early police reports that the father of Vickie Pittman, Vic Pittman, had been implicated as a suspect in her death but never formally charged. Vickie Pittman had had two aunts, Mozelle and Onzelle, who had been collecting information and desperately seeking answers to the questions surrounding their niece's death. They eagerly agreed to talk to us.

Mozelle and Onzelle were two middle-aged, rural white women who were twin sisters. They described themselves as "country tough" and presented themselves as fearless, relentless people who could not be intimidated. They invited us over, sat us at the kitchen table, and wasted no time.

"Did your client kill our baby?" Mozelle asked bluntly.

"No, ma'am, I sincerely believe he did not."

"Do you know who did?"

I sighed. "Well, not completely. We've spoken to Ralph Myers and believe that he and Karen Kelly were involved, but Myers insists that there were others involved as well."

Mozelle looked at Onzelle and leaned back.

"We know there's more involved," said Onzelle. The sisters voiced suspicions about their brother and about local law enforcement. They complained that the prosecutor had disrespected and ignored them.

"They treated us like we were low-class white trash. They could not have cared less about us." Mozelle looked furious as she spoke. "I thought they treated victims better. I thought we had some say."

By the 1980s, a new movement had emerged in the criminal justice system, and there seemed to be an attitude that was more responsive to the perspective of crime victims and their families. The problem was that not all crime victims received the same treatment or respect. As Mozelle and Onzelle discovered, focusing on the social status of the victim became one more way for the criminal justice system to favor some people and disfavor others—specifically poor and minority victims of crime.

Consider the Supreme Court case *McCleskey v. Kemp,* which presented convincing empirical evidence that the race of the victim is the greatest predictor of who gets the death penalty in the United States. The study conducted for that case revealed that offenders in Georgia were eleven times more likely to get the death penalty if the victim was white than if the victim was black. These findings were identical in every other state where studies about race and the death penalty took place. In Alabama, even though 65 percent of all homicide victims were *black,* nearly 80 percent of the people on death row were there for crimes against victims who were *white.* Black defendant and white victim pairings increased the likelihood of a death sentence even more.

Many poor and minority victims, or victims who had family members who were incarcerated, noted that they were not getting calls or support from local police and prosecutors. If your family had lost a loved one to murder or had to suffer the anguish of rape or assault, your victimization might be ignored or taken less seriously. The expansion of victims' rights ultimately made formal what had always been true: some victims are more protected and valued than others.

More than anything else, it was the lack of concern and responsiveness by police, prosecutors, and victims' services providers that devastated Mozelle and Onzelle. "You're the first two people to come to our house and spend time with us talking about Vickie," Onzelle told us. After nearly three hours of hearing their heartbreaking reflections, we promised to do what we could to find out who else was involved in their niece Vickie's death.

We were getting to the point where, without access to police records and files, we wouldn't be able to make more progress. Because the case was now pending on direct appeal to the Alabama Supreme Court, the State had no obligation to let us see those records and files. So we decided to file what is known as a Rule 32 petition, which would put us back in a trial court with the opportunity to present new evidence and obtain discovery, including access to the State files.

Rule 32 petitions are required to include claims that were not raised at trial or on appeal and that could not have been raised at trial or on appeal. They are the vehicle to challenge a conviction based on ineffective counsel, the State's failure to disclose evidence, and most important, new evidence of innocence. Michael and I put a petition together that asserted all of these claims, including police and prosecutorial misconduct, and filed it in the Monroe County Circuit Court.

The document alleged that Walter McMillian was unfairly tried, wrongly convicted, and illegally sentenced—and it drew a lot of attention in Monroeville. Three years had passed since the trial. Most people assumed that Walter's guilt was a fact, and that all there was left to do was wait for an execution date.

Surprisingly, the Alabama Supreme Court agreed to stay (or pause) our direct appeal process so that we could go ahead with the Rule 32 petition. This signaled that the court saw there was something unusual about Walter's case that warranted further review in the lower courts. The Baldwin County Circuit Court judge was now obligated to review our case and could be forced to grant our discovery motions, which would require disclosure of all police and prosecutorial files. This was a very positive development.

We needed to have another meeting with the DA, Tommy

Chapman, and this time we'd be armed with a court order to turn over all files. We would also finally meet, in the flesh, the law enforcement officers involved in Walter's prosecution: the DA's investigator, Larry Ikner; ABI agent Simon Benson; and Sheriff Tom Tate.

When we arrived at Chapman's office in the Monroe County courthouse, the men were already there. Tate was a tall, heavy-set white man who had come to the meeting in boots, jeans, and a light shirt. Ikner was another white man, in his mid-forties, wearing the same outfit. Neither of them smiled much. The men knew that we were accusing them of misconduct.

"How much is Johnny D paying y'all?" Tate asked, using Walter's nickname.

"We work for a nonprofit. We don't charge the people we represent anything," I said as blandly and politely as I could.

"Well, you're getting money from somewhere to do what you do."

I decided to let that pass and move things forward.

"I thought that it might be a good idea to sign something that verifies these are all the files you all have on this case," I said after they handed over their files. I wanted to be certain they gave us *everything*.

"We don't need to do anything that formal, Bryan. These men are officers of the court, just like you and I. You should just take the files," Chapman said, apparently sensing that this suggestion had provoked Tate and Ikner.

"Well, there could be files that have inadvertently been missed or documents that dropped out. I'm just trying to document that what we receive is what you give us—same number of pages, same file folder headings, et cetera. I'm not questioning anyone's integrity."

"The hell you ain't." Tate was direct. He looked at Chapman. "We can sign something confirming what we give him. I think we may need a record of that more than he does."

Chapman nodded. We got the files and left Monroeville with a lot of excitement about what we might find in the hundreds of pages of records we'd received. Back in Montgomery, we eagerly started reviewing.

The files were astonishing. We got records from Taylor Hardin, the mental health facility where Myers was sent after he first refused to testify. We got the ABI file from Simon Benson, the only black ABI agent in South Alabama, as he had proudly told us. We got Monroeville city police department records and other city files. We even got Escambia County records on the Vickie Pittman murder.

Inspired by the elaborate conspiracies that Ralph Myers had described, we soon started asking questions about some of the law enforcement officers whose names kept coming up around the Pittman murder. We even decided to talk to the FBI about some of what we had learned.

It wasn't long after that when the bomb threats started.

CHAPTER EIGHT

All God's Children

UNCRIED TEARS

Imagine teardrops left uncried
From pain trapped inside
Waiting to escape
Through the windows of your eyes

"Why won't you let us out?"
The tears question the conscience
"Relinquish your fears and doubts
And heal yourself in the process."

The conscience told the tears
"I know you really want me to cry
But if I release you from bondage,
In gaining your freedom you die."

The tears gave it some thought
Before giving the conscience an answer

"If crying brings you to triumph
Then dying's not such a disaster."

Ian E. Manuel, Union Correctional Institution

Trina Garnett was the youngest of twelve children living in the poorest section of Chester, Pennsylvania, just outside of Philadelphia. Chester had extraordinarily high rates of poverty, crime, and unemployment—and the worst-ranked public school system among Pennsylvania's 501 districts. Nearly 46 percent of the city's children were living below the federal poverty level.

Trina's father, Walter Garnett, was a former boxer whose failed career had turned him into a violent, abusive alcoholic. Trina's mother, Edith Garnett, was sickly after bearing so many children, some of whom were conceived during rapes by her husband. He would regularly punch, kick, and verbally abuse her in front of the children. When she lost consciousness during the beatings, he would shove a stick down her throat to revive her for more abuse. Nothing was safe in the Garnett home. Trina once watched her father strangle her pet dog into silence because it wouldn't stop barking. He beat the animal to death with a hammer and threw its limp body out a window.

Trina had twin sisters, Lynn and Lynda, who were a year older than she. They taught her to play "invisible" when she was a small child to shield her from their father when he was drunk and prowling their apartment with his belt to beat them. Trina was taught to hide under the bed or in a closet and remain as quiet as possible.

Trina showed signs of intellectual disabilities and other troubles at a young age. When she was a toddler, she became seriously ill after ingesting lighter fluid when she was left unattended. At the age of five, she accidently set herself on fire, resulting in severe burns over her chest, stomach, and back. After weeks in the hospital, she was left terribly scarred. She was nine years old when her mother died.

Soon after that, Trina's father began sexually abusing her older sisters, and they fled. His abuse turned to Trina, Lynn, and Lynda. The girls ran away from home and began roaming the streets of Chester. Trina and her sisters would eat out of garbage cans; sometimes they would not eat for days. They slept in parks and public bathrooms. The girls stayed with their older sister, Edy, until Edy's husband began sexually abusing them. Their older siblings and aunts would sometimes provide temporary shelter, but the living situation would get disrupted by violence or death, and so Trina would find herself wandering the streets again.

Her mother's death, the abuse, and the desperate circumstances all worsened Trina's emotional and mental health problems. She was sometimes so ill her sisters got a relative to take her to the hospital. But she was penniless and was never allowed to stay long enough to become stable or recover.

Late at night in August 1976, fourteen-year-old Trina and

her friend, sixteen-year-old Francis Newsome, climbed through the window of a house to talk to the boys who lived there. The mother of these boys had forbidden her children to play with Trina, but Trina wanted to see them. Once she'd climbed into the dark house, she lit matches to find her way to the boys' room. The house caught fire. It spread quickly, and two boys who were sleeping in the home died from smoke asphyxiation. Their mother accused Trina of starting the fire intentionally, but Trina and her friend insisted that it was an accident.

Trina was traumatized by the boys' deaths and could barely speak when the police arrested her. She was so nonfunctional and listless that her appointed lawyer thought she was incompetent to stand trial. But he failed to file the appropriate motions to support an incompetency determination, which would have pushed the trial back until Trina was well enough to defend herself. Her lawyer (who was later disbarred and jailed for criminal misconduct) also never challenged the State's decision to try Trina as an adult. As a result, Trina was forced to stand trial for second-degree murder in an adult courthouse. At trial, Francis Newsome testified against Trina in exchange for the charges against her being dropped. Trina was convicted of second-degree murder, and the trial moved to the sentencing phase.

Pennsylvania sentencing law was inflexible: the only sentence for those convicted of second-degree murder was mandatory life imprisonment without the possibility of parole. Judge Reed, who presided over the case, expressed serious misgivings about the sentence he was forced to impose, given Trina's devastating life circumstances and the fact that she hadn't intended to harm anyone. "This is the saddest case I've ever seen," he wrote. For a tragic crime committed at fourteen, Trina was condemned to die in prison.

At the age of sixteen, Trina walked through the gates of the State Correctional Institution at Muncy, an adult prison for women, terrified, still suffering from trauma and mental illness and intensely vulnerable—with the knowledge that she would never leave. Prison spared Trina the uncertainty of homelessness but presented new dangers and challenges. Not long after she arrived at Muncy, a male correctional officer pulled her into a secluded area and raped her.

The crime was discovered when Trina became pregnant. As is often the case, the correctional officer was fired but not criminally prosecuted. Trina remained imprisoned and gave birth to a son while handcuffed to a bed. (It wasn't until 2008 that most states abandoned the practice of shackling or handcuffing incarcerated women during delivery.)

Trina's baby boy was taken away from her and placed in foster care. She was devastated, and her mental health deteriorated further. Over the years, she became less functional and more mentally disabled. Her body began to spasm and quiver uncontrollably, until she required a cane and then a wheelchair. By the time she turned thirty, prison doctors diagnosed her with multiple sclerosis, intellectual disability, and mental illness related to trauma.

In 2014, Trina turned fifty-two. She has been in prison for thirty-eight years. She is one of nearly five hundred people in Pennsylvania who have been condemned to mandatory life imprisonment without parole for crimes they were accused of committing when they were between the ages of thirteen and seventeen. It is the largest population of child offenders condemned to die in prison in any single jurisdiction in the world.

In 1990, Ian Manuel and two older boys attempted to rob a couple who were out for dinner in Tampa, Florida. Ian was thirteen years old. When Debbie Baigre resisted, Ian shot her with a handgun given to him by the older boys. The bullet went through Baigre's cheek, shattering several teeth and severely damaging her jaw. All three boys were arrested and charged with armed robbery and attempted homicide.

Ian's appointed lawyer encouraged him to plead guilty, assuring him that he would be sentenced to no more than fifteen years in prison. The lawyer didn't realize that two of the charges against Ian were punishable with sentences of life imprisonment without parole. The judge accepted Ian's plea and then sentenced him to life with no parole. Even though he was thirteen, the judge condemned Ian for living in the streets, for not having good parental supervision, and for his prior arrests for shoplifting and minor property crimes. Ian was sent to an adult prison—the Apalachee Correctional Institution, one of the toughest prisons in Florida. Juveniles housed in adult prisons are five times more likely to be the victims of sexual assault, so the staff at Apalachee put Ian, who was small for his age, in solitary confinement.

Solitary confinement at Apalachee means living in a concrete box the size of a walk-in closet. You get your meals through a slot, you do not see other inmates, and you never touch or get near another human being. If you "act out" by talking back or refusing to follow an order, you are forced to sleep on the concrete floor without a mattress. If you shout or scream, your time in solitary is extended; if you hurt yourself by refusing to eat or mutilating your body, your time in solitary is extended; if you complain to officers or say anything menacing or inappropriate, your time in solitary is extended. You get three showers a week and are allowed forty-five minutes in a small caged area for exercise a few times a week. Otherwise you are alone, hidden away in your concrete box, week after week, month after month.

In solitary, Ian became a self-described "cutter"; he would take anything sharp on his food tray to hurt himself. His mental health unraveled, and he attempted suicide several times. Each time he hurt himself or acted out, his time in isolation was extended.

Ian spent eighteen years in uninterrupted solitary confinement.

Once a month, Ian was allowed to make a phone call. Soon after he arrived in prison, on Christmas Eve in 1992, he used his call to reach out to Debbie Baigre, the woman he shot.

When she answered the phone, Ian spilled out an emotional apology, expressing his deep regret and remorse. Ms. Baigre was stunned to hear from the boy who had shot her, but she was moved by his call. She had physically recovered from the shooting and was working to become a successful bodybuilder and had started a magazine focused on women's health. That first surprising phone call led to a regular correspondence. Ian had been neglected by his family before the crime took place. He'd been left to wander the streets with little parental or family support. In solitary, he met few prisoners or staff. As he sank deeper into despair, Debbie Baigre became one of the few people in Ian's life who encouraged him to remain strong.

After communicating with Ian for several years, Baigre wrote the court and told the judge who sentenced Ian that his sentence was too harsh and that his conditions of confinement were inhumane. She tried to talk to prison officials and gave interviews to the press to draw attention to Ian's plight. "No one knows more than I do how destructive and reckless Ian's crime was. But what we're currently doing to him is mean and irresponsible," she told one reporter. "When this crime was committed, he was a child, a thirteen-year-old boy with a lot of problems, no supervision, and no help available. We are not children."

The courts ignored Debbie Baigre's call for a reduced sentence.

By 2010, Florida had sentenced more than a hundred children to life imprisonment without parole for non-homicide offenses. All of the youngest condemned children—thirteen or fourteen years of age—were black or Latino. Florida had the largest population in the world of children condemned to die in prison for non-homicides.

The section of South Central Los Angeles where Antonio Nuñez lived was plagued by gang violence. Antonio's mother would force her children to the floor when shooting erupted outside their crowded home. Numerous neighbors had been killed after being caught in the cross fire of gun violence.

Antonio's home life was turbulent as well. From the time Antonio was in diapers, he endured beatings by his father, who hit him with his hand, fist, belt, and extension cords, causing bruises and cuts; he also witnessed terrifying conflicts in which his parents would violently assault and threaten to kill each other. Once, he even called the police. He began experiencing severe nightmares from which he awoke screaming. Antonio's depressed mother neglected him; when he cried, she just left him alone. The only activity she could recall ever attending for Antonio was his graduation from a Drug Abuse Resistance Education (DARE) program in elementary school.

In September 1999, a month after he turned thirteen, Antonio Nuñez was riding his bicycle near his home when a stranger shot him in his stomach, side, and arm. Antonio collapsed onto the street. His fourteen-year-old brother, José, heard him screaming and ran to his aid. José was shot in the head and killed. Antonio suffered serious internal injuries that hospitalized him for weeks.

His mother sent him to live with relatives in Las Vegas, where he tried to recover from the tragedy of his brother's death. Antonio was relieved to put the gangs and violence of South Central Los Angeles behind him. He was helpful at home and spent evenings doing his homework with help from his cousin's husband.

But within a year, California probation authorities ordered him to return to Los Angeles. He was on probation for a prior minor offense. In poor urban neighborhoods across the United States, black and brown boys are routinely targeted by the police. Even though many of these kids have done nothing wrong, they are stopped, presumed guilty, and suspected of being dangerous or engaged in criminal activity. The random stops, questioning, and harassment dramatically increase the risk of arrest for petty crimes. Many of these children develop criminal records for behavior that wealthier children engage in without consequences.

Forced back to South Central, Antonio struggled. A court later found that "[l]iving just blocks from where he was shot and his brother was killed, Nuñez suffered trauma symptoms, including flashbacks . . . and an intensified need to protect himself from real or perceived threats." He got his hands on a gun for self-defense but was quickly arrested for it and placed in a juvenile camp. His supervisors reported that he responded positively to the structured environment and guidance of staff members.

After returning from the camp, fourteen-year-old Antonio was invited to a party where two men twice his age let him in on a strange plan: They were planning to fake a kidnapping to get money from a relative who would pay the ransom. They insisted that Antonio join them. The pretend victim sat in the backseat, while the man named Juan Perez drove and Antonio sat in the passenger seat. Before they arrived at their destination to retrieve the money, they found themselves being followed—and then chased—by two Latino men in a gray van. At some point, Perez and the other man gave Antonio a gun and told him to shoot at the van, and a dangerous high-speed shoot-out unfolded. The men chasing them were undercover police officers—but Antonio didn't know that when he fired. When a marked police car joined the pursuit, Antonio dropped the gun just before the car crashed into some trees. No one was injured, but Antonio and Perez were charged with aggravated kidnapping and attempted murder of the police officers.

Antonio and his twenty-seven-year-old codefendant were tried together in a joint trial. Both were found guilty. The Orange County judge sentenced Antonio to imprisonment until death, asserting that he was a dangerous gang member who could never change or be rehabilitated, despite his difficult background and the absence of any significant criminal history. The judge sent him to California's dangerous, overcrowded adult prisons. At fourteen, Antonio became the youngest person in the United States condemned to die in prison for a crime in which no one was physically injured.

Most adults convicted of the kinds of crimes with which Trina, Ian, and Antonio were charged are not sentenced to life imprisonment without parole. So why were these teenagers?

Juvenile justice systems vary across the United States, but most states would have kept Trina, Ian, or Antonio in juvenile custody until they turned eighteen or twenty-one. At most, they might have stayed in custody until age twenty-five or older, if their institutional history or juvenile detention record suggested that they were still a threat to public safety.

In an earlier era, if you were thirteen or fourteen when you committed a crime, you would find yourself in the adult system with a lengthy sentence only if the crime was unusually high-profile—or committed by a black child against a white person in the South. For instance, in the infamous Scottsboro Boys case in the 1930s, two of the defendants, Roy Wright and Eugene Williams, were just thirteen years old when they were wrongfully convicted of rape and sentenced to death in Alabama.

By the late 1980s and early 1990s, the politics of fear and anger sweeping the country and fueling mass incarceration was turning its attention to children. Influential criminologists predicted a new generation of "superpredators." Sometimes expressly focusing on black and brown children, theorists suggested that America would soon be overcome by "elementary school youngsters who pack guns instead of lunches" and who "have absolutely no respect for human life." Across the country, nearly every state created laws to allow children to be prosecuted as adults, thinking that the juvenile justice system wouldn't be harsh enough. Many states lowered or eliminated the minimum age for trying children as adults, leaving children as young as eight vulnerable to adult prosecution and imprisonment.

Tens of thousands of kids who had previously been managed by the juvenile justice system, with its well-developed protections and requirements for children, were now thrown into an increasingly overcrowded, violent, and desperate adult prison system.

The predictions of superpredators proved wildly inaccurate. The juvenile population in America increased from 1994 to 2000, but the juvenile crime rate declined, leading even the academics who had originally supported the superpredator theory to disclaim it. Of course, this admission came too late for kids like Trina, Ian, and Antonio.

When I agreed to represent Trina, Ian, and Antonio years later, they had each been broken by years of hopelessness. Hidden away in adult prisons, they felt unknown and forgotten. With little family support or outside help, they each struggled to survive in dangerous, terrifying environments. There were thousands of children like them scattered throughout prisons in the United States—children who had been sentenced to life imprisonment without parole or other extreme sentences. Soon it became immediately clear that their extreme, unjust sentences were just one of the problems that had to be overcome. They were all damaged and traumatized by our system of justice.

Trina's mental and physical health made life in prison extremely challenging. She was grateful for our help and showed remarkable improvement when we told her that we were going to fight to get her sentence reduced, but she had many other needs. She talked constantly about wanting to see her son. She wanted to know that she was not alone in the world. We tracked down her sisters and arranged a visit where Trina could see her son, and it seemed to strengthen her in ways I wouldn't have thought possible.

I flew to California to meet Antonio at a maximum-security prison dominated by aggressive guards, gangs, and frequent violence. It was an environment that corrupted healthy human development in every way. Reading had always been challenging for Antonio, but he was so determined to learn that he would read a passage over and over, looking up unfamiliar words in the dictionary we sent him. We sent him Darwin's *The Origin of Species,* which he hoped would help him better understand those around him.

It turns out that Ian was very, very bright. Although being

smart and sensitive made his extended time in solitary confinement especially destructive, he had managed to educate himself, read hundreds of books, and write poetry and short stories that reflected an impressive intellect. He sent me dozens of thoughtful letters and poems.

We decided to publish a report to draw attention to the plight of children in the United States who had been sentenced to die in prison. I wanted to photograph some of our clients in order to give the life-without-parole sentences imposed on children a human face. Florida was one of the few states that would allow photographers inside a prison, so we asked prison officials if Ian could be permitted out of his solitary, no-touch existence for an hour so that the photographer we hired could take the pictures. To my delight, they agreed. As soon as the visit with the photographer was over, Ian immediately wrote me a letter.

Dear Mr. Stevenson:

I hope this letter reaches you in good health, and everything is going well for you. The focal point of this letter is to thank you for the photo session with the photographer and obtain information from you how I can obtain a good amount of photos.

As you know, I've been in solitary confinement approx. 14.5 years. It's like the system has buried me alive and I'm dead to the outside world. Those photos mean so very much to me right now. All I have is $1.75

in my inmate account right now. If I send you $1.00 of
that, how many of the photos will that purchase me?

In my elation at the photo shoot today, I forgot to
mention that today June 19th was my deceased mom's
birthday. I know it's not a big significance, but reflecting
on it afterward it seemed symbolic and special that the
photo shoot took place on my mother's birthday!

I don't know how to make you feel the emotion
and importance of those photos, but to be real, I want
to show the world I'm alive! I want to look at those
photos and feel alive! It would really help with my pain.
I felt joyful today during the photo shoot. I wanted it
to never end. Every time you all visit and leave, I feel
saddened. But I capture and cherish those moments in
time, replaying them in my mind's eye, feeling grateful
for human interaction and contact. But today, just the
simple handshake we shared was a welcome addition to
my sensory deprived life.

Please tell me how many photos I can get? I want
those photos of myself, <u>almost</u> as bad as I want my
freedom.

Thank you for making a lot of the positive
occurrences that are happening in my life possible.
I don't know exactly how the law led you to me, but
I thank God it did. I appreciate everything you and EJI
are doing for me. Please send me some photos, okay?

CHAPTER NINE

I'm Here

Finally, the date for Walter McMillian's hearing was nearing. Here was our opportunity to present all the new evidence in Walter's favor, including Ralph Myers's testimony and the newly discovered police records.

Meanwhile, Tom Chapman was preparing to defend Walter's conviction with the help of Assistant Attorney General Don Valeska, a longtime prosecutor with a reputation for being aggressive in his prosecution of "bad guys." Michael and I had reached out to Chapman before the hearing to see if we could persuade him to reopen the investigation and independently reexamine whether Walter McMillian was guilty. But by now, Chapman and all of the law enforcement officers had grown tired of us. I had considered reporting to them the bomb threats and death threats we'd received, since they were likely coming from people in Monroe County, but I wasn't sure anyone in the sheriff's or DA's office would care.

Judge Robert E. Lee Key Jr. had retired. The new judge on

the case, Judge Thomas B. Norton Jr., had also grown weary of us. We kept insisting on obtaining all files and evidence the State had in its possession. We were sure there was still more that had not been turned over.

In the last pretrial appearance, the judge had asked, "How much time will you need to present your evidence, Mr. Stevenson?"

"We'd like to reserve a week, Your Honor."

"A week? You've got to be joking. For a Rule 32 hearing? The trial in this case lasted only a day and a half."

"Yes, sir. We believe this is an extraordinary case and there are several witnesses and—"

"Three days, Mr. Stevenson. If you can't make your case in three days after all this drama you've stirred up, you don't really have anything."

"Judge, I—"

"Adjourned."

After spending another long day in Monroeville tracking down a few final witnesses, Michael and I went back to the office to plan how to present all of the evidence in the narrow amount of time the judge had given us. Another concern was Myers's trustworthiness. Ralph was such a wild card that we didn't know what to expect from him. We sat down with him a few days before the hearing to be crystal clear.

"Just answer the questions accurately and honestly, Ralph," I warned him.

"I always do," Ralph said confidently.

"Wait, did you just say you *always* do?" Michael asked. "What are you talking about, you *always* do? Ralph, you lied through the entire trial. That's what we're going to expose at this hearing."

"I know," Myers said coolly. "I meant I always tell y'all the truth."

"Don't freak me out, Ralph. Just testify truthfully," Michael said.

We arrived at the courthouse the morning of the hearing early and anxious. We were both dressed in dark suits, white shirts, and muted ties. I usually dressed as conservatively as possible for court. I was a young, bearded black man, and I tried to meet the court's expectation of what a lawyer looked like, if only for the sake of my clients.

Both Myers and Walter were in holding cells in the basement of the courthouse. We first went to check on Myers; he was anxious. Worse, he was unusually quiet and reserved. I went to see Walter next. Being back at the courthouse where he'd been convicted four years earlier had shaken him, but he forced himself to smile when I walked in.

"Was the trip okay?" I asked.

"Everything is good. Just hoping for something better than the last time I was here."

I nodded sympathetically and reviewed with him what I thought would unfold over the next few days. Then, I made my way upstairs to get ready for court to begin.

When I entered the courtroom, I was shocked by what I saw. Dozens of people from the community—mostly black and poor, dressed in church clothes—had packed the viewing area. People from Walter's family, people who had attended the fish fry on the day of the crime, people we'd interviewed over the past several months, people who knew Walter from working with him, even Sam Crook and his posse, were crammed into the courtroom. Minnie and Armelia smiled as I walked in.

Tom Chapman then walked in with Don Valeska, and they both scanned the room. I could tell from the looks on their faces that they were unhappy about the crowd. Tate, Larry Ikner, and Benson—the law enforcement team primarily responsible for Walter's prosecution—entered behind them. The parents of Ronda Morrison were seated at the front of the court. It took a few seconds for the black community members to settle into silence, which seemed to annoy Judge Norton, a balding white man in his fifties. But I was energized by their presence and happy for Walter that so many people had come out to support him.

"Gentlemen, are we ready to proceed?" Judge Norton asked.

"We are, Your Honor," I replied. "But we intend to call several of the law enforcement officers present in the courtroom, and I would like to invoke the rule of sequestration."

In criminal cases, witnesses who will be testifying are required to sit outside the courtroom so they can't alter their testimony based on what other witnesses say. Since officers were testifying, it seemed obvious that they should have to sit outside.

Valeska was on his feet immediately. "No, Judge. That's not going to happen. These are the investigators who figured out this heinous crime, and we need them in court to present our case."

I stayed on my feet. "The State doesn't bear the burden of presenting a case in these proceedings, Your Honor; *we* do. This isn't a criminal trial but a postconviction evidentiary hearing."

"Judge, they're the ones that are trying to retry this case and we need our people inside," Valeska countered.

The judge jumped in with "Well, it does sound like you're trying to retry the case, Mr. Stevenson, so I'm going to allow the State to keep the crime investigators in the courtroom."

This was not a good start, but there was nothing we could do. I decided to proceed with an opening statement before calling Myers as our first witness. I wanted the judge to understand that we weren't just defending Mr. McMillian from a different angle than his old lawyers. I wanted him to know that we had dramatic new evidence of innocence that completely cleared Walter. I wanted him to know that justice demanded Walter's immediate release.

"Your Honor, the State's case against Walter McMillian turned entirely on the testimony of Ralph Myers, who had several prior felony convictions and another capital murder case pending against him in Escambia County at the time of Mr. McMillian's trial. At trial, Mr. McMillian asserted that he is innocent and that he did not know Mr. Myers at the time of this crime. He has maintained his innocence throughout these proceedings."

The judge had been fidgeting and had seemed distracted when I started, so I paused. Even if he didn't agree I wanted him to hear what I was saying. I stopped talking until I was sure that he was paying close attention. Finally, he made eye contact with me, so I continued.

"There is no question that Walter McMillian was convicted of capital murder based on the testimony of Ralph Myers. There was no other evidence to establish Mr. McMillian's guilt for capital murder at trial other than Myers's testimony. The State had no physical evidence linking Mr. McMillian to this crime, the State had no motive, the State had no witnesses to the crime, the State had only the testimony of Ralph Myers.

"At trial, Myers testified that he was *unknowingly* and *unwillingly* made part of a capital murder and robbery on November 1, 1986, when Walter McMillian saw him at a car wash and asked him to drive Mr. McMillian's truck because his 'arm hurt.' Myers stated that he drove Mr. McMillian to Jackson Cleaners, subsequently went into the cleaners, and saw Mr. McMillian with a gun, placing money in a brown bag. Another man, who was white, was also present in the cleaners. Myers testified this man had black-gray hair and allegedly talked to

Mr. McMillian. Myers asserted that he was shoved and threatened by Mr. McMillian when he went into the cleaners. The mysterious third person, presumed to be in charge, allegedly instructed Mr. McMillian to 'get rid of Myers,' which Mr. McMillian said he couldn't do because he was out of bullets. The white man in charge has never been identified or arrested by the State. The State has not been looking for a third person, a ringleader for this crime, because I think they recognize that this person doesn't exist."

I paused again to let the meaning of this sink in. "Based on the testimony of Ralph Myers, Walter McMillian was convicted of capital murder and sentenced to death. As you're about to hear, the testimony of Ralph Myers was completely false. Again, Your Honor, the testimony of Ralph Myers at trial was completely false."

I took a moment before turning to the bailiff to call Myers to the stand. The courtroom was silent until the deputy opened the door and Ralph Myers walked into the courtroom. Ralph had aged visibly since the last time the people in the courtroom had seen him; I could hear murmurs about how his hair had grayed. Dressed in his prison whites, Myers once again appeared small and sad to me as he climbed up onto the witness stand. Judge Norton was looking at him attentively.

I walked over to begin my examination. After asking him to state his name for the record and establishing that he had previously appeared in court and testified against Walter McMillian, it was time to get to the heart of things.

I came closer to the witness stand.

"Mr. Myers, was the testimony that you gave at Mr. McMillian's trial true?" I was hoping that the judge couldn't see I was holding my breath waiting for Ralph to answer. Ralph looked at me coolly but then spoke very clearly and confidently.

"Not at all." There was more murmuring in the courtroom now, but the crowd quickly quieted to hear more.

"Not at all," I repeated before continuing. I wanted Ralph's recantation to sink in, but I didn't want to hesitate too long, because we needed a lot more.

"Did you see Mr. McMillian on the day that Ronda Morrison was murdered?"

"Absolutely not." Ralph looked steady as he spoke.

"Did you drive his truck into Monroeville on that day?"

"Absolutely not."

"Did you go into Jackson Cleaners when Ronda Morrison was murdered?"

"No. Never did."

"Now, at Mr. McMillian's trial, did you give some testimony that there was a white man inside the cleaners when you went inside?"

"Yes, I did."

"What was that testimony, please?"

"As I can recall, the testimony was that I had overheard Walter McMillian saying something to this guy, and I also recalled saying that I had seen the back part of his head, but that's just about all I can recall on that."

"Was that testimony true, Mr. Myers?"

"No, it wasn't." Now the judge leaned in to listen with rapt attention.

"Were any of the allegations you made against Walter McMillian as being involved in the Ronda Morrison murder true?"

Ralph paused and looked around the courtroom before he answered. For the first time, there was emotion in his voice, regret or remorse.

"No."

It seemed that everyone in the courtroom had been holding their breath, but now there was an audible buzz from many of Walter's supporters.

I had a copy of the trial transcript and took Ralph through every sentence of his testimony against Walter. Statement by statement he acknowledged that his previous testimony was entirely false. Myers would frequently turn his head to look Judge Norton directly in the eye as he spoke. Even during the lengthy cross-examination by Chapman, he remained firm. After relentless questioning about why he was changing his testimony and Chapman's suggestion that someone was putting him up to this, Ralph became indignant. He looked at the prosecutor and said:

"Me, I can simply look in your face and anybody else's

face dead eye to eyeball and tell you that that's all I—anything that was told about McMillian was a lie. . . . As far as I know, McMillian didn't have anything to do with this because on the day, on the day they say this happened, I didn't even see McMillian. And that's exactly what I told lots of people."

I reviewed my notes and then glanced at Michael to make sure I hadn't forgotten anything. "Are we okay?"

Michael looked astonished. "Ralph was great. He was really, really great."

I looked at Walter and only then realized that his eyes were moist. He was shaking his head from side to side in disbelief. I put my hand on his shoulder before announcing to the court that Myers could be excused. We had no further questions.

Myers stood up to leave the courtroom. As the deputies led him to a side door, he looked apologetically at Walter before being escorted out. I'm not sure Walter saw him.

People in the courtroom started whispering again. I heard one of Walter's relatives, in a muted tone, say, "Thank you, Jesus!"

The next challenge? To disprove the testimonies of Bill Hooks and Joe Hightower, who had claimed to see Walter's modified lowrider truck pulling out from the cleaners about the time Ronda Morrison was murdered.

I called Clay Kast to the stand. The white mechanic testified that Mr. McMillian's truck was not a lowrider in November 1986 when Ronda Morrison was murdered. Kast had records and clearly remembered modifying Walter's truck in May

1987, over six months after the day when Hooks and Hightower claimed they'd seen a lowrider truck at the cleaners.

We finished the day with Woodrow Ikner, a Monroeville police officer who testified that he was the first to arrive at the crime scene on the day of the murder. He asserted that the body of Ronda Morrison was not by the front counter, where Myers had testified it was. More significantly, Ikner testified that he'd been asked by Pearson, the trial prosecutor, to testify that Morrison's body had been dragged through the store from the front counter to the spot where it was found. Ikner knew that such testimony would be false and had told the prosecutors that he refused to lie. He was soon after discharged from the police department.

At this, the judge seemed visibly affected by the proceedings. I believed the concerned look on his face revealed confusion about what he was going to do in light of this evidence, and I considered the judge's newfound confusion and concern to be real progress. This was the first evidence that suggested that people in law enforcement had been so set on convicting Walter that they were ignoring—and even hiding—evidence that showed his innocence. All of the witnesses we called during the first day were white, and none had any loyalties to Walter McMillian. It seemed that Judge Norton had not expected that. The worry lines on his face were deepening. Maybe we were making some progress with him.

When Woodrow Ikner's testimony ended, it was already deep into the afternoon. The judge looked at the clock and called it a day. I wanted to keep going, to continue until midnight if necessary, but I realized that that wasn't going to happen. I walked over to Walter.

"We have to stop now?" he asked worriedly.

"Yes, but we'll just pick up and keep going tomorrow morning." I smiled at him, and I was pleased when he smiled back.

Walter looked at me excitedly. "Man, I can't tell you how I'm feeling right now. All this time I've been waiting for the truth and been hearing nothing but lies. Right now feels incredible. I just—" A middle-aged white officer interrupted us to take Walter back to his holding cell. I told Walter I'd come down later.

As people filed out of the courtroom, you could see hope growing among Walter's family. They came up to me and gave me hugs. Walter's sister Armelia, his wife, Minnie, and his nephew Giles were all talking excitedly about the evidence we'd presented.

Michael was pumped up, too. "Chapman should just call you and say he wants to drop the charges against Walter and let him go home."

"Let's not hold our breath waiting for that call," I replied.

I arrived at the courthouse early the next morning to visit Walter in his basement cell before the proceedings began. When I headed upstairs, I was confused to see a throng of black folks waiting in the courthouse lobby. I went up to Armelia, who looked at me with concern.

"What's wrong?" I asked. "Why aren't y'all inside the courtroom?"

If there had been a huge crowd yesterday, today's hearing had brought more people, including several clergy members and older people of color I'd never seen before.

"They won't let us in, Mr. Stevenson."

"What do you mean, they won't let you in?"

"We tried to go in earlier, and they told us we couldn't come in."

What was going on? I pushed by the deputy, opened the door, and saw that the entire courtroom had been altered. Inside the courtroom door, they had placed a large metal detector, on the other side of which was an enormous German shepherd held back by a police officer. The courtroom was already half filled. The benches that had been filled by Walter's supporters the previous day were now mostly occupied by older white people supporting the Morrisons and the prosecution. Clearly, Chapman and Valeska were trying to keep out Walter's supporters. They were already sitting at the prosecutor's table, acting as if nothing was going on. I was livid.

I went directly to the judge's chambers to explain to Judge Norton that Walter McMillian's family and supporters had been denied entry into the courtroom. He rolled his eyes. "Mr. Stevenson, your people will just have to get here earlier," he said dismissively.

"Judge, the problem isn't that they weren't here early. The problem is they were told they couldn't come into the courtroom."

"No one is being denied entrance to the courtroom, Mr. Stevenson."

He turned to his bailiff, who left the room. I followed the bailiff and saw him whisper something to the deputy outside the courtroom. Mr. McMillian's supporters would be let into the courtroom—now that it was already half-filled.

"I'm sorry, everyone," I explained to the group. "They've done something really inappropriate today. They'll let you in now, but the courtroom is already half-filled with people here to support the State. There won't be enough seats for everyone."

There were two ministers in the group. One of them, a heavyset African American man dressed in a dark suit with a large cross around his neck, walked over to me. "Mr. Stevenson, it's okay. Please don't worry about us. We'll have a few people be our representatives today and we will be here even earlier tomorrow. We won't let nobody turn us around, sir."

Minnie, Armelia, Walter's children, and several others went in. When the ministers called out, "Mrs. Williams," everyone seemed to smile. Mrs. Williams, an older black woman, stood up and prepared herself to enter the courtroom. She precisely adjusted the placement of her small hat, and delicately wrapped a long blue scarf around her neck.

I was thrilled to see all of Mr. McMillian's supporters but realized that I needed to go inside myself. I hadn't spent the morning preparing for witnesses as I had intended but had instead been drawn into this foolish mistreatment of Walter McMillian's supporters.

I was standing at counsel's table when out of the corner of my eye I saw that Mrs. Williams had made it to the courtroom door. She wasn't a large woman, but there was something commanding about her presence—I couldn't help but watch her as she moved toward the metal detector. She walked more slowly than everyone else, but she held her head high with an undeniable grace and dignity. She reminded me of older women I'd been around all my life—women whose lives were hard but who remained kind and dedicated themselves to building and sustaining their communities. Mrs. Williams glanced at the available rows to see where she would sit, and then turned to walk through the metal detector—and that's when she saw the dog.

I watched all her composure fall away, replaced by a look of absolute fear. Her shoulders dropped, her body sagged, and she seemed paralyzed. For over a minute she stood there, frozen, and then her body began to tremble and then shake noticeably. I heard her groan. Tears were running down her face and she began to shake her head sadly. Then she turned around and hurried out of the courtroom.

. . .

I was trying to shake off the dark feeling that the morning's events had conjured when the officers brought Walter into the courtroom. They allowed him to be in the courtroom without handcuffs but had insisted on keeping his ankles shackled.

Despite the State's early-morning maneuvers and the bad omen of the dog and Mrs. Williams, we had another good day in court. State mental health workers who had treated Myers confirmed his testimony from the day before. Dr. Omar Mohabbat explained that Myers had told him then "that the police had framed him to accept the penalty for the murder case that he is accused of or 'to testify' that 'the man did.'" Mohabbat reported that Myers also told him, "'They told me to say what they wanted me to say.'"

Evidence from three other doctors further confirmed this testimony, including a Dr. Bernard Bryant, who testified that Myers told him "he did not commit the crime and that at the time he was incarcerated for the crime, he was threatened and harassed by the local police authorities into confessing he committed a crime."

We emphasized to the court that all of these statements were made by Myers *before* the initial trial. Not only did these statements boost the credibility of Myers's recantation but they had also been documented in medical records that, by law, should have been turned over to Walter's trial lawyers.

The State's supporters and the victim's family seemed confused by the evidence we were presenting—it complicated the simple narrative they had embraced about Walter's guilt and the need for swift and harsh punishment. We had maintained a good pace and the cross-examinations had been shorter than I had expected. By the end of that second day, I felt very hopeful.

I was tired but feeling pleased as I walked to my car that evening. To my surprise, I noticed Mrs. Williams, the older woman from that morning, sitting outside the courthouse on a bench, alone. She stood when our eyes met. I walked over, remembering how unsettled I had been to see her flee from the courtroom earlier.

"Mrs. Williams, I'm so sorry they did what they did this morning. They should not have done it and I'm sorry if they upset you. But, so you know, things went well today. I feel like we had a good day—"

"Attorney Stevenson, I feel so bad. I feel so bad," she said and grabbed my hands. "I should have come into that courtroom this morning." She began to weep.

"Mrs. Williams, it's all right," I said. "They shouldn't have done what they did. Please don't worry about it." I put my arm around her and gave her a hug.

"No, no, no, Attorney Stevenson. I was meant to be in that courtroom. I was supposed to be in that courtroom."

"It's okay, Mrs. Williams, it's okay."

"No, sir, I wanted to be there. I tried, I tried, Lord knows I tried, Mr. Stevenson. But when I saw that dog—" She shook her head and stared away with a distant look. "When I saw that dog, I thought about 1965, when we gathered at the Edmund Pettus Bridge in Selma and tried to march for our voting rights. They beat us and put those dogs on us." She looked back to me sadly. "I tried to move, Attorney Stevenson, I wanted to move, but I just couldn't do it."

As she spoke, it seemed like a world of sadness surrounded her. She let go of my hand and walked away. I watched her get into a car with some other people I had seen in the courtroom earlier.

I drove back to the motel in a more somber mood to start preparing for the last day of hearings.

The next morning was the third and final day of the hearing. The metal detector and the dog were still there, but no deputy stood at the door to block black people from entering.

When I looked up at the courtroom door, there stood Mrs. Williams. She was once again dressed impeccably in her scarf and hat. I watched as the officers allowed her to move forward. She held her head up as she walked slowly through the metal detector, repeating over and over, "I ain't scared of no dog, I ain't scared of no dog." It was impossible to look away. She made it through the detector and stared at the dog. Then, loud enough for everyone to hear, she belted out: "I ain't scared of no dog!"

She moved past the dog and walked into the courtroom. Black folks who were already inside beamed with joy as she passed them. She sat down near the front of the courtroom and turned to me with a broad smile and announced, "Attorney Stevenson, I'm here!"

"Mrs. Williams, it's so good to see you here. Thank you for coming."

The courtroom filled up, and I started getting my papers together. They brought Walter into the courtroom, the signal that the hearing was about to begin. That's when I heard Mrs. Williams call my name.

"No, Attorney Stevenson, you didn't hear me. I said I'm here." She spoke very loudly, and I was a little confused and embarrassed. I turned around and smiled at her.

"No, Mrs. Williams, I did hear you, and I'm so glad you're here." When I looked at her, though, it was as if she was in her own world.

The courtroom was packed, and the bailiff brought the court to order as the judge walked in. Everyone rose, as is the custom. When the judge took the bench and sat down, everyone else in the courtroom sat down as well. There was an unusually long pause as we all waited for the judge to say something. I noticed people staring at something behind me, and that's when I turned around and saw that Mrs. Williams was still standing. The courtroom got very quiet. All eyes were on her. I tried to gesture to her that she should sit, but then she leaned her head back and shouted, "I'm here!" People chuckled nervously as she took her seat, but when she looked at me, I saw tears in her eyes.

In that moment, I felt something peculiar, a deep sense of recognition. I smiled now, because I knew she was saying to the room, "I may be old, I may be poor, I may be black, but I'm here. I'm here because I've got this vision of justice that compels me to be a witness. I'm here because I'm supposed to be here. I'm here because you can't keep me away."

I smiled at Mrs. Williams while she sat proudly. For the first time since I started working on the case, everything we were struggling to achieve finally seemed to make sense. It took me a moment to realize that the judge was calling my name, impatiently asking me to begin.

The last day of hearings went well. Six people who had been jailed or imprisoned with Ralph Myers testified that Ralph had told them he was being pressured to give false testimony against Walter McMillian. Their testimonials were consistent, and one explained that Myers had written letters saying he didn't even know Mr. McMillian.

We saved the most powerful evidence for the end: the tapes of Thomas Tate, Simon Benson, and Larry Ikner interrogating Myers. On the tapes, Myers repeatedly told the police that he didn't know anything about the Morrison murder or Walter

McMillian. The officers threatened Myers, and Myers resisted framing an innocent man for murder.

Not only did the recordings confirm Myers's recantation, they exposed the lie that Pearson had told the court, the jury, and Mr. McMillian's trial counsel—that there were only two statements provided by Myers. In fact, Myers gave at least six additional statements to the police. They were all favorable to Walter McMillian, and none of them had been disclosed to Mr. McMillian's attorneys, as was required.

I called on Mr. McMillian's trial lawyers, Bruce Boynton and J. L. Chestnut, to testify about how much more they could have done to win an acquittal—a not-guilty verdict—if the State had turned over the evidence it had suppressed.

We finished the presentation of our evidence and, to our surprise, the State put on no rebuttal case. I didn't know what they could have presented to deny our evidence, but I'd assumed they would present *something*. The judge seemed surprised, too. He paused and then said he wanted the parties to submit written briefs arguing what ruling he should make. We had hoped for this, and I was relieved that the court would give us time to explain the significance of all the evidence in writing and assist him in preparing his order, an order I hoped would set Walter free.

At the end of three days of intense litigation, Michael and I said our farewells to the family in the courtroom and left feeling exhausted but satisfied.

. . .

Bay Minette, where the hearing took place, is about thirty minutes from the beautiful beaches on the Gulf of Mexico. We had started a tradition of bringing our staff down to the beach each September, and we'd all fallen in love with the clear, spectacular waters of the gulf. Dolphins could be spotted in the early mornings, playfully making their way through the water. I'd often thought we should move our office to right there on the water.

It was Michael's idea to hit the beach after the hearing before heading back to Montgomery. I wasn't sure it was a good idea, but the day was warm and the coast was so close, I couldn't resist. It would soon be dusk, but the heat persisted. I stood at the water's edge, my head racing with everything that had transpired in court: I replayed what witnesses had said and worried about whether things had gone exactly right. I analyzed every detail in my mind, every possible misstep, until I caught myself. It was over; there was no point in making myself crazy by overthinking it now.

On the sandy shore, I watched the brilliant white pelicans gliding effortlessly over the still waters in search of food. Walter would be making his way back to Holman now, shackled in the back of the van again. I thought about his family and all the people who had come to court. They'd kept the faith through the five years that had passed since Walter was first arrested. I thought about Mrs. Williams. She had come up to me after the hearings and had given me a sweet kiss on the cheek. I told her how happy I was she'd come back to court. She looked at me playfully. "Attorney Stevenson, you *know* I wasn't going to let these people keep me out." Her words had made me smile.

Michael got out of the water looking worried.

"What did you see?" I joked. "Shark? Eel? Poisonous jelly-fish? Stingray? Piranha?"

He was out of breath. "They've threatened us, lied to us, there are people who have told us that some folks in the county are so unnerved by what we're doing that they're going to kill us. What do you think they're going to do now that they know how much evidence we have to prove Walter's innocence?"

I had given this some thought, too. Our opponents had done everything they could to frame Walter—in order to kill him. They'd lied to us and subverted the judicial process. More than a few people had told us that they'd heard angry people in the community make threats on our lives because they believed we were trying to help a guilty murderer get off death row.

"I don't know," I told Michael, "but we have to press on, man, we have to press on."

We both sat there in silence, watching the sun fade into darkness.

CHAPTER TEN

Mitigation

America's prisons have become warehouses for the mentally ill. Mass incarceration has been largely fueled by misguided drug policy and excessive sentencing, but the internment of hundreds of thousands of poor and mentally ill people has been a driving force in achieving our record levels of imprisonment. It's created unprecedented problems. For over a century, Americans suffering from serious mental illness have been shifted between prisons and mental institutions. In the late nineteenth century, alarmed by inhumane treatment of mentally ill people in prison, Dorothea Dix and Reverend Louis Dwight led a successful campaign to get mentally ill people out of prison. As a result, state mental hospitals started opening up to provide care for the mentally distressed.

But by the middle of the twentieth century, abuses within these mental hospitals began generating a lot of attention. Families, teachers, and courts were sending thousands of people to institutions for "issues" like resisting social, cultural, or sexual norms—not for acute mental illness. People who were gay, transgender, or engaged in interracial dating found themselves committed against their will.

In the 1960s and 1970s, laws were enacted to prevent involuntary commitment. People with developmental disabilities were empowered to refuse treatment. Forced institutionalization became much less common. By the 1990s, several states had reduced the patient count in mental hospitals by more than 95 percent.

While these reforms were desperately needed, the timing of them intersected with the spread of mass imprisonment policies—expanding criminal statutes and harsh sentencing—and the effects were disastrous. The "free world" became perilous for deinstitutionalized poor people suffering from serious mental disabilities, such as schizophrenia or psychosis. Disabled low-income people who could not afford to receive treatment or necessary medication were greatly at risk of a police encounter that would result in jail or prison time. Jail and prison had already become the State's strategy for dealing with a health crisis created by drug use and dependency. Now, on top of that, a flood of mentally ill people headed to prison for minor offenses and drug crimes, or simply for behaviors their communities were unwilling to tolerate.

Today, over 50 percent of prison and jail inmates in the United States have a diagnosed mental illness. In fact, there are more than three times the number of seriously mentally ill individuals in jail or prison than in hospitals; in some states, that number is ten times. And prison is a terrible place for someone with mental illness or a neurological disorder that prison guards are not trained to understand.

For instance, when I still worked in Atlanta, our office sued Louisiana's notoriously rough Angola Prison for refusing to modify a policy that required prisoners in segregation cells to place their hands through bars for handcuffing before officers entered to move them. Disabled prisoners with epilepsy and seizure disorders would sometimes need assistance while convulsing in their cells, and because they couldn't put their hands through the bars, guards would Mace them or use fire extinguishers to subdue them. This intervention aggravated the health problems of the prisoners and sometimes resulted in death.

Most prisons are overcrowded and don't have the capacity to provide care and treatment to the mentally ill. Without treatment, complying with the many rules of prison life is impossible for many disabled people. Other prisoners exploit or react violently to their behavioral symptoms. Frustrated prison staff frequently subject them to abusive punishment, solitary confinement, or the most extreme forms of detention. Many judges, prosecutors, and defense lawyers do a poor job of recognizing the special needs of the mentally disabled, which leads to wrongful convictions, lengthier prison terms, and high rates of returns to prison after release.

. . .

A lot of my clients on death row have had serious mental illnesses. For some, mental illness has developed in prison, as a result of stress and trauma. But Avery Jenkins's letters, handwritten in print so small I needed a magnifying glass to read them, convinced me that he had been very ill for a long time.

I looked up his case and began to piece together his story. It turned out he'd been convicted of the very disturbing and brutal murder of an older man. The multiple stab wounds inflicted on the victim strongly suggested mental illness, but the court records and files never referenced anything about Jenkins suffering from a disability. I thought I'd find out more by meeting him in person.

When I pulled into the prison parking lot, I noticed a pickup truck there that looked like a shrine to the Old South: it was completely covered with disturbing bumper stickers, Confederate flag decals, and other troubling images about guns and Southern identity. One read, IF I'D KNOWN IT WAS GOING TO BE LIKE THIS, I'D HAVE PICKED MY OWN DAMN COTTON. Despite growing up around images of the Confederate South and working in the Deep South for many years, I was pretty shaken by the symbols.

I'd always been especially interested in the post-Reconstruction era of American history. My grandmother was the daughter of people who were enslaved. She was born in Virginia in the 1880s, after federal troops had been withdrawn and a reign of terror had begun, designed to deprive African Americans of any political or social rights. Her father told her stories about how the promise of freedom and equality following slavery ended immediately as white Southerners reclaimed their political power through violence. Recently emancipated black people were essentially re-enslaved by former Confederate officers and soldiers, who used intimidation, lynching, and peonage (forced labor to pay off debts) to keep African Americans subordinate and marginalized.

Terrorist groups like the Ku Klux Klan cloaked themselves in the symbols of the Confederate South to intimidate and victimize thousands of black people. For a hundred years, any sign of black progress in the South could trigger a white reaction that included Confederate symbols and threats. In the 1950s and 1960s, civil rights activism and new federal laws inspired the same resistance to racial progress and once again led to a spike in the use of Confederate imagery. In fact, it was in the 1950s, after racial segregation in public schools was declared unconstitutional in *Brown v. Board of Education,* that many Southern states erected Confederate flags atop their state government buildings.

At a pretrial hearing, I once argued against the exclusion of African Americans from the jury pool. After presenting the data and making my arguments about the unconstitutional exclusion of African Americans, the judge complained loudly.

"I'm going to grant your motion, Mr. Stevenson, but I'll be

honest. I'm pretty fed up with people always talking about minority rights. African Americans, Mexican Americans, Asian Americans, Native Americans . . . When is someone going to come to my courtroom and protect the rights of Confederate Americans?" I wanted to ask if being born in the South or living in Alabama made me a Confederate American, but I thought better of it.

I stopped in the prison yard to take a closer look at the truck, walking around it and reading the stickers and symbols of racial oppression. As I entered the prison, I was met by a correctional officer I'd never seen before. He was a white man of my height—about six feet tall—with a muscular build. He looked to be in his early forties and wore a short military haircut. He was staring coldly at me with steel-blue eyes. I walked toward the gate that led to the lobby of the visitation room, where I expected a routine pat-down before meeting Avery Jenkins in the visitation area. The officer stepped in front of me and blocked me from proceeding.

"What are you doing?" he snarled.

"I'm here for a legal visit," I replied. "It was scheduled earlier this week. The people in the warden's office have the papers." I smiled and spoke as politely as I could to defuse the situation.

"That's fine, that's fine, but you have to be searched

first. . . . You're going to go into that bathroom and take everything off if you expect to get into my prison."

I was shocked but spoke as nicely as I could. "Oh, no, sir. I think you might be confused. I'm an attorney. Lawyers don't have to get strip-searched to come in for legal visits."

Instead of calming him, this seemed to make him angrier. "Look, I don't know who you think you are, but you're not coming into my prison without complying with our security protocols. Now, you can get into that bathroom and strip, or you can go back to wherever you came from."

I'd had some difficult encounters with officers getting into prisons from time to time, mostly in small county jails or places where I'd never been before, but this was highly unusual.

"I've been to this prison many times, and I've never been required to submit to a strip search. I don't think this is the procedure," I said more firmly.

"Well, I don't know and don't care what other people do, but this is the protocol I use," he snapped.

I had driven two hours for this visit and had a very tough schedule over the next three weeks; I wouldn't be able to get back to the prison any time soon if I didn't get in now. I went inside the bathroom and removed my clothes. The officer came in and gave me an unnecessarily aggressive search before mumbling that I was clear. I put my suit back on and walked out.

"I'd like to get inside the visitation room now." I tried to reclaim some dignity by speaking more forcefully.

"Well, you have to go back and sign the book."

He said it coolly, but he was clearly trying to provoke me. I'd already signed the attorney book. It would make no sense to sign a second book.

"Lawyers don't have to sign that book—"

"If you want to come in my prison, you'll sign the book." He seemed to be smirking now. I tried hard to keep my composure, turned around, and signed my name.

I walked back to the visitation room and waited until the officer finally pulled out his keys to unlock the door. When he opened the door, I stepped forward, but he grabbed my arm to stop me. He lowered his voice as he spoke.

"Hey, man, did you happen to see a truck out in the visitation yard with a lot of bumper stickers, flags, and a gun rack?" His face hardened. "I want you to know, that's my truck." Then he released my arm and allowed me to walk inside the prison. I felt angry at the guard, but I was even more irritated by my own powerlessness. I was distracted from my thoughts when the back door of the visitation room opened and Mr. Jenkins was led in by another officer.

Jenkins was a short African American man with close-cropped hair. He grasped my hand with both of his and smiled broadly as he sat down. He seemed unusually happy to see me.

"Mr. Jenkins, my name is Bryan Stevenson. I'm the attorney you spoke—"

"Did you bring me a chocolate milk shake?" He spoke quickly.

"I'm sorry, what did you say?"

He kept grinning. "Did you bring me a chocolate milk shake? I want a chocolate milk shake."

The trip, the Confederate truck, the harassment from the guard, and now a request for a milk shake—this was becoming a bizarre day. I didn't hide my impatience.

"No, Mr. Jenkins, I didn't bring you a chocolate milk shake. I'm an attorney. I'm here to help you with your case and try to get you a new trial. Okay? That's why I'm here. Now I need to ask you some questions and try to understand what's going on."

I saw the grin fade quickly from the man's face. I started asking questions and he gave single-word answers, sometimes just grunting out a yes or no. I realized that he was still thinking about his milk shake. My frustration with the officer had made me forget how impaired this man might be. I stopped the interview and leaned forward.

"Mr. Jenkins, I'm really sorry. I didn't realize you wanted me to bring you a chocolate milk shake. If I had known that, I would absolutely have tried. I promise that the next time I come, if they let me bring you in a chocolate milk shake, I'll definitely do it. Okay?"

With that, his smile returned, and his mood brightened. He was generally kind and gentle in our meeting, but he was clearly ill. His prison records revealed that he often experienced psychotic episodes in which he would scream for hours. His trial records made no reference to mental illness.

When I returned to my office, we began a deeper investigation into Mr. Jenkins's background. What we found was heartbreaking. His father had been murdered before he was born, and his mother had died of a drug overdose when he was a year old. He'd been in foster care since he was two years old and it had been horrific: nineteen different foster homes before he turned eight. Many of the families that had taken him in were physically and sexually abusive. He began showing signs of intellectual disability at an early age. He had cognitive impairments that suggested some organic brain damage and behavioral problems that suggested schizophrenia and other serious mental illness.

By the time he was thirteen, he had started abusing drugs and alcohol. By fifteen, he was having seizures and experiencing psychotic episodes. At seventeen, he was left homeless. Avery was in and out of jail until he turned twenty, when in the midst of a psychotic episode he wandered into a strange house, thinking he was being attacked by demons. In the house, he brutally stabbed to death a man he'd believed to be a demon. His lawyers did no investigation of Mr. Jenkins's history prior to trial, and he was quickly convicted of murder and sentenced to death.

The prison would not let me bring Mr. Jenkins a milk shake. I tried to explain this to him, but at the start of every visit, he'd ask me if I'd brought one. I promised that I would keep trying—I had to, just to get him to focus on anything else.

Months later, we were finally scheduled to go to court to

present the material that his lawyers should have presented at trial: evidence about his profound mental illness. Before the hearing started, I went to see Avery in the court's basement holding cell. After going through my usual protocol about the milk shake, I tried to get him to understand what would happen in court. I was concerned that seeing some of the witnesses—people who had dealt with him when he was in foster care—might upset him. Also, the testimony the experts would provide would be very direct in characterizing his disabilities and illness. I wanted him to understand why we were doing that. He was pleasant and agreeable, as always.

Upstairs in the courtroom, I spotted the correctional officer who had given me such a hard time when I had first met Avery. I hadn't seen him since that initial ugly encounter—he must have been the officer assigned to transport Avery to the hearing. I had asked another client about the guard and was told that he had a bad reputation. Most people tried to steer clear of him.

Over the next three days, we presented our evidence about Avery's background. The medical experts who spoke about Avery's disabilities were terrific. They explained how organic brain damage, schizophrenia, and bipolar disorder can create severe mental impairment. They explained that the psychosis and other serious mental health problems that Mr. Jenkins had could lead to dangerous behavior. This dangerous behavior stemmed from serious illness; it was not a reflection of his character. We also put forth evidence of how the foster care system had failed Avery. Several of the foster parents with whom Avery had been placed were later convicted of sexual abuse and criminal mismanagement of foster children. We discussed how Avery had been passed from one dangerous situation to the next, until he was drug-addicted and homeless.

Several of Avery's former foster parents admitted to being very frustrated by him because they didn't know how to deal with his severe mental health problems. I argued to the judge that not taking Avery's mental health issues into consideration at trial was as cruel as saying to someone who has lost his legs, "You must climb these stairs with no assistance, and if you don't, you're just lazy."

There are hundreds of ways we accommodate physical disabilities—or at least understand them. But because mental disabilities aren't visible in the same way, we tend to be dismissive of them, and quick to judge. Brutally murdering someone would, of course, require the State to hold that person accountable and to protect the public. But to completely disregard a person's disability would be unfair in deciding what degree of culpability to assign and what sentence to impose.

I went back home feeling very good about the hearing, but I wasn't expecting any miracle rulings. About a month after the hearing, before judgment was rendered, I decided to go to the prison and see if Avery was okay.

When I pulled into the parking lot, I once again saw that loathsome truck, with its flags, stickers, and gun rack. Sure enough, as I headed toward the visitation room, I saw the guard approaching me. I braced myself, preparing for the encounter. And then something surprising happened.

"Hello, Mr. Stevenson. How are you?" the guard asked. He sounded earnest and sincere, and he wasn't glaring at me for once. I was skeptical but I decided to play along.

"Well, I'm fine. Look, I'll step into the bathroom to get ready for your search."

"Oh, Mr. Stevenson, you don't have to worry about that," he quickly replied. "I know you're okay." Everything about his tone and demeanor was different.

"Oh, well, thank you. I appreciate that. I'll go back and sign the book, then."

"Mr. Stevenson, you don't have to do that. I saw you coming and signed your name in for you. I've taken care of it." I realized that he actually looked nervous.

Confused, I thanked him and walked to the visitation room door with the officer following behind me. He turned to unlock the padlock so that I could go inside. Before I could enter, he placed his hand on my shoulder.

"Hey, um, I'd like to tell you something."

I wasn't sure where he was going with this.

"You know I took ole Avery to court for his hearing and was down there with y'all for those three days. And I, uh, well, I want you to know that I was listening." He removed his hand from my shoulder and looked past me, as if staring at something behind me. "You know, I—uh, well, I appreciate what you're doing, I really do. It was kind of difficult for me to be in that courtroom to hear what y'all was talking about. I came up in foster care, too." His face softened. "Man, I didn't think anybody had it as bad as me. They moved me around like I wasn't wanted nowhere. I had it pretty rough. But listening to what you was saying about Avery made me realize that there were other people who had it as bad as I did. I guess even worse. I mean, it brought back a lot of memories, sitting in that courtroom."

He reached into his pocket to pull out a handkerchief to wipe perspiration from his brow. I noticed for the first time that he had a Confederate flag tattooed on his arm.

"You know, I guess what I'm trying to say is that I think it's good what you're doing. I got so angry coming up that there were plenty of times when I really wanted to hurt somebody, just because I was angry. I made it to eighteen, joined the military, and you know, I've been okay. But sitting in that courtroom brought back memories, and I think I realized how I'm still kind of angry."

I smiled. He continued: "That expert doctor you put up said that some of the damage that's done to kids in these abusive homes is permanent; that kind of made me worry. You think that's true?"

"Oh, I think we can always do better," I told him. "The bad things that happen to us don't define us. It's just important sometimes that people understand where we're coming from."

Another officer walked by and stared at us. I went on:

"You know, I really appreciate you saying to me what you just said. It means a lot, I really mean that. Sometimes I forget how we all need mitigation at some point."

He looked at me and smiled. "You kept talking about mitigation in that court. When I got home I looked it up. I wasn't sure what you meant at first, but now I do . . . I think you done good, real good." He looked me in the eye before he extended his hand. We shook hands and I started toward the door. I was just about inside when he grabbed my arm again.

"Oh, wait. I've got to tell you something else. Listen, I did something I probably wasn't supposed to do. On the trip back down here after court . . . well, I took him to a Wendy's, and I bought him a chocolate milk shake."

I stared at him incredulously, and he broke into a chuckle. Then he left me inside the room. I was so stunned by what the officer said, I didn't hear the other officer bring Avery into the room. When I realized Avery was there, I turned and greeted him. When he didn't say anything, I was a little alarmed.

"Are you okay?"

"Yes, sir, I'm fine. Are you okay?" he asked.

"Yes, Avery, I'm really doing well." I waited for our ritual to begin. When he didn't say anything, I figured I'd just play my part. "Look, I tried to bring you a chocolate milk shake, but they wouldn't—"

Avery cut me off. "Oh, I got a milk shake. I'm okay now."

As I began discussing the hearing, he grinned. We talked for an hour before I had to see another client. Avery never again asked me for a chocolate milk shake. We won a new trial for him and ultimately got him off death row and into a facility where he could receive mental health treatment. I never met the officer again; someone told me he quit not long after that last time I saw him.

CHAPTER ELEVEN

I'll Fly Away

It was the third bomb threat in two months. As we quickly cleared the office and waited for the police to arrive, the entire EJI staff—five attorneys, an investigator, law school interns, and three administrative staff members—were nervous. None of them had signed on for bomb threats.

It was tempting to ignore them, but two years earlier an African American civil rights lawyer in Savannah, Georgia, named Robert "Robbie" Robinson was murdered when a bomb sent to his law office exploded. Around the same time, a federal appeals court judge, Robert Vance, was killed in Birmingham by a mail bomb. Days later a third bomb was sent to a civil rights office in Florida and a fourth to a courthouse in Atlanta. The bomber seemed to be attacking legal professionals connected to civil rights. We were warned that we could be targets, and for weeks we carefully hauled our mail packages to the federal courthouse for X-ray screenings before opening them. After that, bomb threats were no joke.

Everyone fled the building while we discussed the likelihood of an actual bombing. The caller had described our building precisely when making his threat. Sharon, our receptionist, said the man had sounded middle-aged and Southern, but she couldn't give any more of a description. It wasn't his first time calling. "I'm doing you a favor," he said threateningly. "I want y'all to stop doing what you're doing. My first option is not to kill everybody, so you better get out of there now! Next time, there won't be a warning."

Although I was handling other cases, I was certain the calls were in response to the McMillian case. Michael and I had been followed several times while doing investigative work in Monroe County. I got threatening calls at home. One typical caller said, "If you think we're going to let you help that lowlife get away with killing that girl, you've got another thing coming. You're both going to be dead!" It was hard to know how seriously to take any of it, but it was definitely unnerving.

After we cleared the building, the police went through the office with dogs. No bomb was found, and when the building didn't blow up after an hour and a half, we all filed back inside. We had work to do.

A few days later, a call came in from the clerk's office in Baldwin County. The clerk was calling to let me know that Judge Norton had ruled in the McMillian case—she needed my fax number to send me a copy of the ruling. I waited nervously by the fax machine. When only three sheets of paper came through the machine, I was concerned.

The pages contained a tersely worded order from Judge Norton denying us relief. After all that, Walter's death penalty conviction remained. I had suspected that this would be Judge Norton's response. For all his interest at the hearing, he had never seemed particularly interested in the basic question of whether Walter was guilty or innocent.

What was surprising, however, was how superficial and thoughtless the court's two-and-a-half-page order read. The judge addressed only Ralph Myers's testimony and none of the many legal claims we'd presented or any of the testimonies of the other dozen-plus witnesses.

I was disappointed but not hopeless. There was a next step: we could bring our evidence to the Alabama Court of Criminal Appeals. We were now regularly arguing cases in front of that court, and they were starting to respond to our advocacy. We had won four reversals in death penalty cases in 1990, four more in 1991, and by the end of 1992, we'd won relief for another eight death row prisoners. Though the court was often resistant, we persisted and continued raising serious errors in capital cases.

I was optimistic that we could win relief for Mr. McMillian on appeal. Even if the court was unwilling to rule that Walter was innocent and should be released, the withholding of exculpatory evidence (evidence in his favor) was extreme enough that the case would likely require a new trial. I explained to

Walter that with the Alabama Court of Criminal Appeals, we were only just now getting to a court where our claims would be seriously considered.

At this time, Michael had been hired as a San Diego federal public defender. He agonized about leaving EJI, but he was ready to leave Alabama. One of our new attorneys, Bernard Harcourt, replaced him on Walter's case. Bernard was a lot like Michael in that he was smart, determined, and extremely hardworking. He had been preparing for a traditional legal career, until he came down to work with us one summer and became fascinated by the issues that death penalty cases presented. He quickly immersed himself in Walter's case.

The crowd at Walter's hearing got the community talking about what we had presented in court. More people started coming forward with helpful information, and claims of police corruption and misconduct. Bernard and I continued to track leads and interview people in Monroe County.

Not everyone was swayed by the hearing, though. Local Monroeville and Mobile newspapers printed claims that Walter was a "drug kingpin," a "sexual predator," and a "gang leader." Despite all of the evidence presented at our hearing showing that Walter had nothing to do with the Pittman murder, the local press used it to scare up more fear about him. The narrative in the press was clear: this man was extremely dangerous.

The threats we received made me worry about the hostility that Walter would face if he was ever released. I wondered how safely he could live locally, if everyone outside his community was persuaded that he was a dangerous murderer.

The case was now pending in the Court of Criminal Appeals. If the public could only know what we knew, it might ease his reentry into freedom. We wanted people to understand this simple fact: *Walter did not commit that murder.*

Could some positive media attention help our case? I wasn't so sure. In fact, the chief judge on the court, John Patterson, had famously sued the *New York Times* over their coverage of the civil rights movement when he was Alabama's governor. It was a common tactic used by Southern politicians during civil rights protests: accuse newspapers of trying to ruin their reputations—even sue them for defamation if they provided sympathetic coverage of civil rights activists, or if they critiqued Southern politicians and law enforcement officers.

I had no doubt that national press coverage of Walter's case would *not* help our cause at the Court of Criminal Appeals. My general attitude was that press coverage rarely helped our clients. Beyond the general anti-media sentiments in the South, the death penalty was a politically charged topic. Even sympathetic pieces about people on death row usually triggered a backlash that created more problems for the client and the case. But I did think getting a more informed view of Walter's conviction and the murder would convince some locals that he was innocent and—assuming we could ever get his conviction overturned—make his life after release less dangerous.

It was risky, but we felt that we had to take our chances and get the story out.

Journalist Pete Earley jumped into the case, spent time with several of the involved individuals, and quickly came to share our astonishment that Walter had been convicted on such unreliable evidence.

That year, I'd given a speech at Yale Law School that was attended by a producer from the popular CBS investigative program *60 Minutes,* and he also called me. We filed our appeal in the Court of Criminal Appeals that summer, and with no small amount of lingering uncertainty, I decided to move forward with the *60 Minutes* piece. Veteran reporter Ed Bradley and his producer, David Gelber, came down from New York City to Monroeville on a 100-degree day in July and interviewed many of the people whose testimony we'd presented at our hearing. They spoke with Walter, Ralph Myers, Karen Kelly, Darnell Houston, Clay Kast, Jimmy Williams, Walter's family, and Woodrow Ikner. They confronted Bill Hooks at his job and interviewed Tommy Chapman extensively.

When the *60 Minutes* piece aired months later, local officials and local media outlets were quick to discredit it, claiming that it was further injuring Ronda Morrison's parents. Writers at local newspapers complained that the new publicity "could lead many people to think McMillian is innocent."

But people in the community watched *60 Minutes* all the time and generally trusted it. Despite the local media reaction, the CBS coverage gave the community a summary of the evidence we'd presented in court and created questions and doubts about Walter's guilt.

People in the black community, who had been discussing Walter's wrongful conviction for years, were thrilled to see honest coverage of the case. We frequently got calls from people simply seeking an update, or a clarification of a particular point that had been the subject of debate in a barbershop or at a social gathering. For many black people in the region, watching the evidence that we had presented in court now laid out on national television was therapeutic.

It turned out that, privately, District Attorney Tom Chapman had started worrying about the reliability of the evidence against Walter. Given our success in other death penalty cases, he must have feared that the court might indeed overturn Walter's conviction. Chapman had become the public face defending the conviction, and he realized that he'd put his own integrity on the line by relying on the work of local investigators—work that was now revealed as almost laughably flawed.

Chapman called together Tate, Larry Ikner, and Benson

shortly after the hearing to ask them to explain the contradictory evidence we had presented. He wasn't impressed with what he heard. Finally, he decided to ask ABI officials in Montgomery to reexamine the evidence and conduct another investigation into the murder to confirm Mr. McMillian's guilt—something we'd been asking him to do for more than two years.

Chapman never told us directly that he was starting another investigation. We found out about it when the new investigators from the ABI, Tom Taylor and Greg Cole, called me. After meeting with them, I was even more hopeful about what might come out of the investigation. They were not connected to any of the players in South Alabama. They both seemed no-nonsense, experienced, and interested in doing honest and reliable work.

We gave them all our case files and evidence. We had nothing to hide. I was confident that any reasonable, honest investigation would reveal the absurdity of the charges against Walter.

By January, six months had passed since we had filed our appeal at the Court of Criminal Appeals, and a ruling was due any week. That's when Tom Taylor called and said that he and Cole wanted to meet with us again. We'd talked a few times during their investigation, but this time we'd finally be discussing their findings. When they arrived, Bernard and I sat down with them in my office and they wasted no time.

"There is no way Walter McMillian killed Ronda Morrison."

Tom Taylor spoke plainly and directly. "We're going to report to the attorney general, the district attorney, and anyone who asks that McMillian had nothing to do with either of these murders and is completely innocent."

I tried not to look as thrilled as I felt. I didn't want to scare away this good news. "That's terrific," I said, trying to sound unsurprised. "I'm pleased to hear that and I have to say I'm extremely grateful that you've looked at the evidence in this case thoroughly and honestly."

"Well, confirming that McMillian had nothing to do with this wasn't that hard," Taylor replied. "What we were told by local law enforcement about McMillian didn't make much sense, and the story Myers told at trial definitely made no sense. I still can't believe a jury ever convicted him."

Cole spoke up. "You'll be very interested to know that both Hooks and Hightower have admitted that their trial testimony was false."

"Really?" I couldn't hide my surprise at this.

"Yes. When we were asked to investigate this case, we were told that you should be investigated because Hooks had said that you had offered him money and a condo in Mexico if he changed his testimony." Taylor was dead serious.

"A condo in Mexico?"

"On a beach, I think," Cole added nonchalantly.

"Wait, *me*? I was going to give Bill Hooks a beach condo in Mexico if he changed his testimony against Walter?" It was difficult to contain my shock.

"Well, I know it must sound crazy to you, but believe me, there were people down there who were raring to get you indicted. But when we talked to Hooks, it didn't take very long before he not only acknowledged that he'd never spoken to you and that you had never bribed him, but he also admitted that his trial testimony against McMillian was completely made up."

"We've never had any doubts that Hooks was lying," I noted.

Cole chuckled. "We started polygraphing people, and things fell apart pretty quickly."

Bernard asked the obvious question: "What happens now?"

Taylor looked over at his partner and then at us. "Well, we're not completely done. We'd like to solve this crime. I'm wondering if you might be willing to help us. I know you're not trying to get anybody on death row, but we thought you might consider providing some help to identify the real killer. People will be a lot more accepting of Mr. McMillian's innocence if they know who really committed this crime."

While it was ridiculous to think that Walter's freedom depended on someone else's arrest, we had long ago concluded that finding the real murderer might be the most effective way to free him. Without law enforcement officers on our side, though, we were limited in what we could uncover.

Here's what we had so far: Several witnesses had told us that around the time of the crime, they'd seen a white man leaving the cleaners. We had learned that before her death, Ronda Morrison had been receiving menacing calls and that there was a man who had been inappropriately pursuing her—stopping by unannounced at the cleaners, maybe even stalking her. We had not been able to identify this strange man.

But we did have our suspicions. A white man who seemed intensely interested in the case contacted us frequently to ask about the investigation. He would hint at having information that could help, and repeatedly told us he would help prove that Walter McMillian was innocent. He even claimed to know where the murder weapon, which had never been recovered, might be located.

We researched the caller's background and discovered a history of stalking, violence against women, and preoccupation with the Morrison murder. We began to think that our caller could be the person who had murdered Ronda Morrison. We had dozens of phone conversations with him and even met him a couple of times. Once we asked him direct questions about where he was on the day of the murder, which must have alarmed him, because we heard from him less often after that.

Before I could tell any of this to the ABI investigators, Taylor named our suspect. I told Taylor to give us a few days to organize the information and recordings of phone calls, and then we would turn it over.

"We want to get Walter out of prison as soon as possible," I insisted.

"Well, I think the attorney general and the lawyers would like to maintain the status quo for a few more months, until we can make an arrest of the actual killer."

"Right, but you do understand that the status quo is a problem for us? Walter has been on death row for nearly six years for a crime he didn't commit."

Taylor and Cole looked at each other uncomfortably. Taylor admitted, "If I was in prison for something I didn't do and you were my lawyer, I hope you'd get me out as soon as you could."

When they left, Bernard and I were very excited, but we remained troubled by this plan to "maintain the status quo." I was furious that the State would try to prolong any order granting relief to Walter. It was consistent with everything that had happened over the last six years, but it was still maddening. We told the court that there was overwhelming evidence that Mr. McMillian's rights had been violated, and that he was entitled to immediate relief. Delaying relief would add further injury to a man who had been wrongfully convicted and condemned to death row for a crime he did not commit.

I was talking to Minnie and the family every week now, keeping everyone updated about the new State investigation.

"I feel like something good is about to happen, Bryan," Minnie said to me. "They've kept him for years. Now it's time they let him go. They have to let him go."

I appreciated her optimism, but I worried, too. We'd been disappointed so often before.

Managing the family's expectations was a complex task. I felt I was supposed to be the cautionary voice that prepared family members for the worst even while I urged them to hope for the best. Increasingly, I was recognizing the importance of hopefulness in creating justice.

On February 23, nearly six weeks after getting the ABI's report, I received a call from the clerk of the court. The Court of Criminal Appeals had ruled in the McMillian case and we could pick up the opinion.

"You're going to like this," she said mysteriously.

I *ran* to the courthouse. By the time I sat down to read the thirty-five-page ruling, I was out of breath. The clerk was right. The ruling invalidated Walter's conviction and death sentence. The court didn't conclude that he was innocent and must be released, but it ruled in our favor on every other claim and ordered a new trial.

I didn't realize how much I had feared that we would lose until we finally won.

I jumped into the car and raced down to death row to tell Walter in person. I watched him take it all in. He leaned back and gave me a familiar chuckle.

"Well," he said slowly, "you know, that's good. That's good."

"Good? It's great!"

"Yeah, it is great." He was grinning now with a freedom

I hadn't seen before. "Whew, man, I can't believe it, I can't believe it. . . . Whew!"

His smile started to fade, and he began slowly shaking his head.

"Six years, six years gone." He looked away with a pained expression. "These six years feel like fifty. Six years, just gone. I've been so worried they were going to kill me, I haven't even thought about the time I've lost."

His troubled look sobered me, too. "I know, Walter, and we're not clear yet," I said. "The ruling only gives you a new trial. Given what the ABI has said, I can't believe they would try to prosecute you again, but with this crowd, reasonable conduct is never guaranteed. I'm going to try and get you home as soon as humanly possible."

With thoughts of home, his mood lightened and we started talking about things we'd been too afraid to discuss since we'd met. He said, "I want to meet everybody who has helped me in Montgomery. And I want to go around with you and tell the world what they did to me. There are other people here who are as innocent as I am." He paused and started smiling again. "Man, I want some good food, too. I ain't had no real good food in so long that I can't even remember what it tastes like."

"Whatever you want, it will be my treat," I said proudly.

"From what I hear, you might not be able to afford the kind of meal I want," he teased. "I want steak, chicken, pork, maybe some good cooked coon."

We relaxed and laughed a lot. We had laughed before

that—Walter's sense of humor hadn't failed him despite his six years on death row. But the laughter that day felt very different. It was the laughter of liberation.

I drove back to Montgomery and thought about how to speed up Walter's release. I called Tommy Chapman and told him that I intended to file a motion to dismiss all charges against Walter in light of the appellate court ruling. I asked if he would consider joining the motion, or at least not opposing it. He sighed. "I'll get back to you about whether I'll join it. We certainly won't oppose it."

The State did, in fact, join our motion to dismiss the charges. A final hearing on the motion was set, and it wouldn't last more than a few minutes.

Walter would finally be able to walk out of the courthouse a free man.

The night before the hearing, I drove down to Minnie's to get a suit for Walter to wear to the courthouse. When I arrived at her house, she gave me a long hug. It looked like she had been crying and hadn't slept. We sat down, and she told me again how happy she was that they were letting him out. But she looked troubled. Finally, she turned to me.

"Bryan, I think you need to tell him that maybe he shouldn't come back here. It's just all been too much. The stress, the gossip, the lies, everything. He doesn't deserve what they put him through, and it will hurt me to my heart the rest of my life what they did to him, and the rest of us. But I don't think I can go back to the way things were."

"Well, you all should talk when he gets home."

"We want to have everybody over when he gets out. We want to cook some good food, and everybody will want to celebrate. But after that, maybe he should go to Montgomery with you," she said.

I had already talked with Walter about not staying his first few nights in Monroeville, for security reasons. We had talked about him spending time with family members in Florida while we monitored the local reaction to his release. But I hadn't discussed his future with Minnie.

I drove back to Montgomery, sadly realizing that even as we stood on the brink of victory and what should have been a glorious release for Walter and his family, this whole nightmare— the conviction, the death sentence, and the heartbreak and devastation of this miscarriage of justice—would likely never be completely over for him.

State, local, and national media outlets were crowded outside the courthouse when I arrived the next morning. Dozens of Walter's family members and friends from the community were there to greet him when he came out. They had made signs and banners, which surprised me. They were such simple gestures, but I found myself deeply moved. The signs gave a silent voice to the crowd: "Welcome Home, Johnny D," "God Never Fails," "Free at Last, Thank God Almighty, We Are Free at Last."

I went down to the jail and brought Walter his suit. I told him that a celebration was planned at his house after the hearing. The prison had not allowed Walter to bring his possessions to the courthouse, refusing to acknowledge that he might be released, so we would have to go back to Holman Prison to get his things before the homecoming meal. I also told him that I'd reserved a hotel room for him in Montgomery and that it would probably be safest to spend the next few nights there.

I reluctantly talked to him about my conversation with Minnie. He seemed surprised and hurt but didn't linger on it.

"This is a really happy day for me. Nothing can really spoil getting your freedom back."

"Well, y'all should talk at some point," I urged.

I went upstairs to find Tommy Chapman waiting for me in the courtroom. "After we're done, I'd like to shake his hand," he told me. "Would that be all right?"

"I think he'd appreciate that," I said.

"This case has taught me things I didn't even know I had to learn," Chapman said.

"We've all learned a lot, Tommy."

Everyone was strangely pleasant. Judge Norton had retired weeks before the ruling, and the new judge, Pamela Baschab, greeted me warmly. "Mr. Stevenson, I don't need any

arguments or statements. I intend to grant the motion immediately so you all can get home. We can get this done quickly,"
she said.

There was no metal detector, no menacing dog. The courtroom was packed with Walter's family members and supporters. There were more cheering black folks outside the
courthouse who couldn't get in. A horde of television cameras
and journalists spilled out of the crowded courtroom.

They finally brought Walter into the courtroom, wearing
the black suit and white shirt I'd brought him. The deputies
didn't handcuff Walter or shackle him, so he walked in waving
to family and friends. Many in the crowd gasped. His family
had not seen him dressed in anything but his white prison uniform in six years. He looked handsome and fit, like a different
man.

The judge took the bench, and I stepped forward to speak.
I gave a brief history of the case and informed the court that
both the defendant and the State were moving the court to
dismiss all charges. The judge quickly granted the motion and
asked if there was anything further. Everyone was suddenly
generous and accommodating. It was as if they wanted to be
sure there were no hard feelings or grudges.

I felt strangely agitated. We were about to leave court for
the last time, and I started thinking about how much pain and
suffering had been inflicted on Walter, his family, the entire
community. I thought about how if Judge Robert E. Lee Key
Jr. hadn't overridden the jury's verdict of life imprisonment

without parole and imposed the death penalty, which is what brought the case to our attention, Walter likely would have spent the rest of his life incarcerated and died in a prison cell. I thought about how certain it was that hundreds, maybe thousands of other people were just as innocent as Walter but would never get the help they need. I knew this wasn't the time to make a speech, but I couldn't stop myself from making one final comment.

"Your Honor," I spoke up. "I just want to say this before we adjourn. It was far too easy to convict this wrongly accused man for murder and send him to death row for something he didn't do and much too hard to win his freedom after proving his innocence. We have serious problems and important work that must be done in this state."

I sat down and the judge pronounced Walter free to go. Just like that, he was a free man.

Walter hugged me tightly, and I gave him a handkerchief to wipe the tears from his eyes. Graciously, Walter agreed to shake Chapman's hand. I asked Bernard to tell the family and supporters that we would meet them out front.

Walter stood very close to me as we answered questions from the press. I could tell he was feeling overwhelmed, so I cut off the questions after a few minutes. TV camera crews followed us as we exited the courthouse. Outside, dozens of people cheered and waved their signs. Walter's relatives ran up to hug him, and they hugged me, too. Walter's grandchildren grabbed his hands. Walter couldn't believe how many people were there for him. Even when some of the men came up to shake his hand, he gave them a hug. I told everyone that Bernard and I had to take Walter to the prison to pick up his things and that we would come to the house directly from there.

On the drive to the prison, Walter told me that the men on death row had held a special service for him on his last night. They had come to pray for him and give him their final hugs. Walter said he felt guilty leaving them behind. I told him not to—they were all thrilled to know he was going home. His freedom was, in a small way, a sign of hope in a hopeless place.

We went to the prison office to collect Walter's possessions: his legal materials and correspondence with me, letters from family and supporters, a Bible, the Timex watch he was wearing when he was arrested, and the wallet he had had with him back in June 1987 when his nightmare began. The wallet still had twenty-three dollars in it. Walter had given to other death row prisoners his fan, a dictionary, and the food items he had in his cell.

A few guards watched as we walked out the front gate of the prison. Members of the press and people from Walter's family and community had followed our car to the prison. Lots of people were gathered outside. I saw Mrs. Williams. Walter went up to her and gave her a hug. She looked over and winked at me. I couldn't help but laugh.

Men in their cells could see the crowd outside and started shouting encouragement to Walter as he walked away. We couldn't see them from outside the prison, but their voices rang out just the same—the voices were haunting because they were disembodied, but they were full of excitement and hopefulness. One of the last voices we heard was a man shouting, "Stay strong, man. Stay strong!"

Walter shouted back, "All right!"

As he walked to the car, Walter raised his arms and gently moved them up and down as if he meant to take flight. He looked at me and said, "I feel like a bird, I feel like a bird."

CHAPTER TWELVE

Mother, Mother

Marsha Colbey and her husband, Glen, may have been poor, but they always gave their family all of their love. A white woman from a rural Alabama town, forty-three-year-old Marsha already had six kids when she discovered she was pregnant with a seventh. Marsha knew that a pregnancy at her age was very risky, but she couldn't afford to see a doctor. One day while she was taking a bath, she went into labor extremely early and gave birth to a stillborn son. She desperately tried to revive the infant, but he never took a breath. The baby's stillbirth might have remained a private tragedy for Marsha and her family had it not been for a nosy neighbor who had long been suspicious of the Colbeys.

Debbie Cook noticed that Marsha Colbey was no longer pregnant but did not have a baby, which stirred her interest. Cook involved the police in hopes that they would investigate the "absent" infant. Unbelievably, Marsha Colbey—a few short weeks after delivering her stillborn son—soon found herself arrested and charged with capital murder.

The jury on Mrs. Colbey's case returned a verdict of guilty on one count of capital murder. The trial court sentenced her to life imprisonment without the possibility of parole, and a short while later, she found herself shackled in a prison van heading to the Julia Tutwiler Prison for Women.

Between 1990 and 2005, a new prison opened in the United States every ten days. Prison growth and the "prison-industrial complex"—the business interests that capitalize on prison construction—made imprisonment profitable. Incarceration became the answer to everything. Health care problems like drug addiction? Poverty that led someone to write a bad check? Child behavioral disorders? Managing the mentally disabled? Undocumented immigration? The solution according to legislators was to send people to prison. Never before had so much lobbying money been spent to expand America's prison population, block sentencing reforms, create new crime categories, and sustain the fear and anger that fuel mass incarceration than during the last twenty-five years in the United States.

In the United States, the number of women sent to prison increased 646 percent between 1980 and 2010. With close to two hundred thousand women in jails and prisons in America and over a million women under the supervision or control of the criminal justice system, the incarceration of women has reached record levels.

Most incarcerated women—nearly two-thirds—are in prison for nonviolent, low-level drug crimes or property crimes. Drug laws in particular have had a huge impact on the number of women sent to prison; so have "three strikes" laws, which seriously increase sentences for people who have previous convictions.

At the time of Marsha Colbey's arrest, all five of the women who were on Alabama's death row were condemned for the unexplained deaths of their young children or the deaths of abusive spouses or boyfriends—all of them. In fact, nationwide, most women on death row are awaiting execution for a family crime involving an allegation of child abuse or domestic violence involving a male partner.

The murder of a child by a parent is horrific and is usually complicated by serious mental illness. But these cases also tend to create distortions and bias. Police and prosecutors have been influenced by the media coverage, and a presumption of guilt has now fallen on thousands of women—particularly poor women in difficult circumstances—whose children die unexpectedly. In a nation that spends more on health care than any other country in the world, the inability of many poor women to get adequate health care, including prenatal and postpartum care, has been a serious problem in this country for decades. The criminalization of infant mortality and the persecution of poor women whose children die have taken on new dimensions in twenty-first-century America, as prisons across the country began to bear witness.

In addition to unexplained deaths of infants, poor women have also been criminalized for other kinds of "bad parenting." In 2006, Alabama passed a law that made it a felony to expose a child to a "dangerous environment" in which the child could encounter drugs. Ostensibly, this measure was passed to protect children living in households where there were meth labs or drug-trafficking operations. But the law was applied much more broadly, and soon thousands of mothers with children living in poor, marginalized communities where drugs and drug addiction are rampant were at risk of being prosecuted.

In time, the Alabama Supreme Court interpreted the term *environment* to include the womb and the term *child* to include a fetus. Pregnant women could now be criminally prosecuted and sent to prison for decades if there was any evidence that they had used drugs at any point during their pregnancy. Dozens of women have been sent to prison under this law in recent years, rather than getting the help they need.

Built in the 1940s, Tutwiler Prison is situated in Wetumpka, Alabama. Named after Julia Tutwiler, a woman who promoted the education of prisoners and championed humane conditions of confinement, Tutwiler has become the opposite of what its namesake stood for: a dangerous nightmare for the women trapped there. Courts have repeatedly found the prison unconstitutionally overcrowded, with almost twice the number of women incarcerated as it was designed to hold.

I had started challenging conditions of confinement at Tutwiler in the mid-1980s as a young attorney with the Southern Prisoners Defense Committee. At the time, I was shocked to find women in prison for such minor offenses. One of the first incarcerated women I ever met was a young mother who was serving a long prison sentence for writing checks to buy her three young children Christmas gifts without sufficient funds in her account. None of the checks was for more than $150. She was not unique. Thousands of women have been sentenced to lengthy terms in prison for writing bad checks or for minor property crimes that trigger mandatory minimum sentences.

The collateral consequences of incarcerating women are significant. Approximately 75 to 80 percent of incarcerated women are mothers with minor children. Nearly 65 percent had minor children living with them at the time of their arrest—children who have become more vulnerable and at risk as a result of their mother's incarceration and will remain so for the rest of their lives, even after their mothers come home.

In 1996, Congress passed legislation that needlessly included a provision that authorized states to ban people with drug convictions from public benefits and welfare. This misguided law greatly affects the lives of formerly incarcerated women with children, most of whom were imprisoned for drug crimes. These women and their children can no longer live in public housing, receive food stamps, or access basic services. In the last twenty years, we've created a new class of "untouchables" in America, made of up our most vulnerable mothers and children.

Marsha wandered through her first days at Tutwiler in a state of disbelief. She met other women like herself who had been imprisoned after having given birth to stillborn babies. Efernia McClendon, a young black teenager from Opelika, Alabama, got pregnant in high school and didn't tell her parents. She delivered at just over five months and left the stillborn baby's remains in a drainage ditch. When they were discovered, she was interrogated by police until she acknowledged that she couldn't be 100 percent sure the infant hadn't moved before death, even though the premature delivery made that *extremely* unlikely. Threatened with the death penalty, she, too, was imprisoned for having an unplanned pregnancy and little access to health care.

After we met Marsha Colbey, we immediately began working on her appeal. We decided to challenge the State's case and the way the jury had been selected. Charlotte Morrison, a Rhodes Scholar and former student of mine, was now a senior attorney at EJI. She and staff attorney Kristen Nelson met with Marsha repeatedly. Marsha would talk about her case, the challenge of keeping her family together while she was in prison, and a range of other problems. But it was the sexual violence at Tutwiler that most frequently came up during these visits.

Women at Tutwiler were being raped, sexually harassed, exploited, and abused by male prison guards in countless ways. The male warden allowed the male guards entry into the showers during prison counts. Officers leered at the naked women and made crude comments and suggestive threats. Women had no privacy in the bathrooms, where male officers could watch them use the toilet. There were dark corners and hallways—terrifying spaces at Tutwiler where women could be beaten or sexually assaulted. EJI had asked the Department of Corrections to install security cameras in the dorms, but they refused. The culture of sexual violence was so pervasive that even the prison chaplain was sexually assaulting women when they came to the chapel.

Charlotte and I took on the case of another woman who had filed a federal civil suit after she was raped at Tutwiler. The details of her experience were so painful that we could no longer look past the violence. We started an investigation for which we interviewed over fifty women; we were truly shocked to see how widespread the problem of sexual violence had become. Several women had been raped and become pregnant. Even when DNA testing confirmed that male officers were the fathers of these children, very little was done about it. Some officers were temporarily reassigned to other duties or other prisons, only to wind up back at Tutwiler, where they continued to prey on inmates. We eventually filed a complaint with the US Department of Justice and released several public reports about the problem, which received widespread media coverage. Tutwiler made it onto a list of the ten worst prisons in America, compiled by *Mother Jones.* Legislative hearings and policy changes at the prison followed. Male guards are now banned from the shower areas and toilets, and a new warden has taken over the facility.

Marsha held on despite these challenges and started advocating for some of the younger women. We were devastated when the Court of Criminal Appeals issued a ruling affirming her conviction and sentence. We sought review in the Alabama Supreme Court and won a new trial based on the trial judge's refusal to exclude people from jury service who were biased and could not be impartial. Marsha and our team were thrilled, local officials in Baldwin County less so. They were threatening re-prosecution. We involved expert pathologists and persuaded local authorities that there was no basis on which to convict Marsha of murder. It took two years to settle the legal case and then another year of wrangling with the Department of Corrections before Marsha was finally freed in December 2012—after ten years of wrongful imprisonment.

On the day of her release from Tutwiler, Marsha had come to the EJI office to thank everyone. Her husband and her two daughters had picked her up at Tutwiler. Her youngest daughter, who was about twelve, had reduced most of our staff to tears because she refused to let go of her mother the entire time. She clung to Marsha's waist, kept hold of her arm, and leaned into her as if she intended never to let anyone physically separate them ever again. We took pictures with Marsha and some of the staff, and her daughter is in every shot because she refused to let her mother go. That told us a lot about what kind of mom Marsha Colbey was.

CHAPTER THIRTEEN

Recovery

E vents in the days and weeks following Walter's release
were completely unexpected. The *New York Times* covered his exoneration in a front-page story. We were flooded
with media requests, and Walter and I gave television interviews to local, national, and even international press. I still
hoped that if people in Monroe County heard enough reports
that Walter had been released because he was innocent, there
would be less resistance to accepting his return home.

Walter was not the first person to be released from death
row after being proved innocent. Several dozen innocent people who had been wrongly condemned to death row had been
freed before him. The Death Penalty Information Center reported that Walter was the fiftieth person to be exonerated
since 1976. Yet few of the earlier cases drew much media attention.

Around the time of Walter's release, media was covering
the death penalty more and more, triggered by an increase in

executions. In 1992, the year before his release, thirty-eight people were executed in the United States—the highest number in a single year since the beginning of the modern death penalty era in 1976, and the numbers kept going up (there were ninety-eight executions in 1999). Walter's case complicated the debate in very graphic ways; politicians and law enforcement officials wanted more and faster executions, but here was an innocent man who had nearly been killed.

As we talked to media and gave interviews, Walter remained calm and jovial, and it was very effective—watching him tell his story with such good humor, intelligence, and sincerity heightened the horror our audiences felt, that the State had been determined to execute this man in all of our names.

Walter would occasionally share with me that he was still troubled by the cases of the men he'd left behind on death row. He thought of the guys on the row as his friends. Walter had become fiercely opposed to capital punishment, an issue he admitted he had never thought about until his own experience confronting it.

A few months after winning his freedom, I was still nervous about Walter's return to Monroe County. Following his release, hundreds of people came to his home to celebrate his freedom, but I knew that not everyone in the community was overjoyed. I didn't tell Walter about the death threats and bomb threats we'd received until he was free, and then I told him that we needed to be careful. He spent his first week out of prison in Montgomery. He then moved to Florida to live with his sister for a couple of months. We still talked almost every day. He'd accepted that Minnie wanted to move forward without him and seemed mostly happy and hopeful.

But that didn't mean there were no aftereffects from his time in prison. He opened up more and more about how unbearable it had been to live under the constant threat of execution on death row. He admitted fears and doubts he hadn't told me about when he was incarcerated. He had witnessed six men leave for execution while he was on the row. At the time of the executions, he coped as the other prisoners did—through symbolic protests and private anguish. But he told me that he didn't realize how much the experience had terrified him until he left prison. He was confused about why that would bother him now that he was free.

"Why do I keep thinking about this?"

He sometimes complained of nightmares.

All I could tell him was that it would get better.

After a few months, Walter very much wanted to return to the place he'd spent his whole life. It made me nervous, but he went ahead and put a trailer on property he owned in Monroe County and resettled there. Meanwhile, we made plans to file a civil lawsuit against everyone involved in his wrongful prosecution and conviction.

Most people released from prison after being proved innocent receive no money, no assistance, no counseling—nothing from the state that wrongly imprisoned them. Even today, almost half of all states (twenty-two) offer no compensation to the wrongly imprisoned to help them get back on their feet, or even to make up for money they would have been making during the time they were incarcerated.

At the time Walter was set free, Alabama was not among the handful of states that provided aid to innocent people released from prison. The local press reported that he was seeking $9 million from the state. Some of Walter's friends and family started soliciting him aggressively for financial help. Walter at times expressed frustration that people didn't believe him when he told them he had received nothing.

We pressed ahead in our efforts to get compensation for Walter through a lawsuit, but there were obstacles. Police, prosecutors, and judges were protected by laws that gave them special immunity from civil liability in criminal justice matters, which would otherwise have required them to pay Walter for damages. So even though it was clear that Ted Pearson, the prosecutor who brought the case against Walter, had illegally withheld evidence that directly resulted in Walter's wrongful prosecution and conviction, we would likely not succeed in a civil action against him.

We sued almost a dozen state and local officials and agencies. After a year of depositions, hearings, and pretrial litigation, we eventually reached a settlement that would provide Walter with a few hundred thousand dollars. Walter's claim against Monroe County for Sheriff Tate's misconduct could not be settled, though, so we appealed the case to the US Supreme Court. After many frustrating challenges, we ultimately reached settlement with all parties, but I was disappointed that we couldn't get more for Walter. Adding insult to injury, Tate went on to be reelected sheriff.

While the money wasn't as much as we would have liked, it did allow Walter to restart his logging business. He loved getting back into the woods and cutting timber. Working from morning until night, being outdoors, made him feel normal again. Then one afternoon, tragedy struck. He was cutting a tree, when a branch dislodged and struck him, breaking his neck. He didn't have a lot of care available, so he came to live with me in Montgomery for several months until he recovered. Sadly, he could no longer cut trees and perform difficult landscape work. I marveled at how he seemed to take it in stride.

"I'll figure out something else to do when I get back on my feet," he told me.

After a few months, he returned to Monroe County and started collecting car parts for resale. He owned the plot of land where he'd put his trailer and had become convinced, on the advice of some friends, that he could generate income with a junk business—collecting discarded vehicles and car parts and reselling them. The work was less physically demanding than logging and allowed him to be outdoors. Before long, his property was littered with busted vehicles and scrap metal.

In 1998, Walter and I were asked to go to Chicago to attend a national conference where exonerated former death row prisoners were planning to gather. By the late 1990s, the evolution of DNA evidence had helped expose dozens of wrongful convictions. Concerns about innocence and the death penalty were intensifying, and support for the death penalty in opinion polls began to drop. Walter seemed more motivated than ever to talk about his experience.

Around the same time, I started teaching at the New York University School of Law. I would travel to New York to teach my classes and then fly back to Montgomery to run EJI. Walter came to New York each year to talk to my class. He usually spoke very briefly, but he had an enormous effect on the students. He would laugh and joke and tell them he wasn't angry or bitter, just grateful to be free. He would share how his faith had helped him survive his hundreds of nights on death row.

One year, Walter got lost on the trip to New York, and he called to tell me that he couldn't make it. He seemed confused and couldn't offer a coherent explanation of what had happened at the airport. When I got back home, I went to see him and he seemed his usual self, just a little down. He told me that his junkyard business wasn't going great, that running the business cost more than he made from selling goods. After an hour or two of anxious talk, he relaxed a bit and seemed to return to the jovial Walter I'd come to know. We agreed that we would travel together on any future trips.

. . .

In 1994, a conservative majority took power in Congress, cutting funding for legal aid to death row prisoners. We scraped along and found enough private support to continue our work, though many groups like ours were forced to close. Our staff was overextended, but I was thrilled with the talented lawyers and professionals we had working with us. We were assisting clients on death row, challenging excessive punishments, helping disabled prisoners, assisting children incarcerated in the adult system, and looking at ways to expose racial bias, discrimination against the poor, and the abuse of power. It was overwhelming but gratifying.

One day, I received a surprising call from the Swedish ambassador to the United States, who told me that EJI had been selected for the Olof Palme Prize, an international human rights award. They sent a film crew to interview me a month or two before the trip I was to take to accept the award, and the crew also wanted to speak with a few clients. I made arrangements for them to interview Walter.

I'd always been with Walter when he spoke to the press, but I hoped he'd be fine alone. "He doesn't give speeches. He's usually very direct," I told the interviewers. "And it's probably better if you talk to him outside, too. He prefers to be outdoors." They nodded sympathetically but seemed confused by my anxiety. Later, over the phone, Walter reassured me that the interview had gone fine.

When I watched the film weeks later, I saw myself walking with the reporter into Dr. Martin Luther King Jr.'s church on Dexter Avenue in Montgomery, then up the street to the Civil Rights Memorial. The scene then switched to Walter, standing in overalls amid his pile of discarded cars down in Monroeville.

Walter gently put down a little kitten he'd been holding as he started to answer the reporters' questions. He said things I'd heard him say dozens of times before. Then I watched his expression change, and he began talking with more animation and excitement than I'd ever heard from him.

He became uncharacteristically emotional. "They put me on death row for six years! They threatened me for six years. They tortured me with the promise of execution for six years. I lost my job. I lost my wife. I lost my reputation. I lost my—I lost my dignity."

He was speaking loudly and passionately and looked to be on the verge of tears. "I lost everything," he continued. He calmed himself and tried to smile, but it didn't work. He looked soberly at the camera. "It's rough, it's rough, man. It's rough." I watched worriedly while Walter crouched down close to the ground and began to sob violently. The camera stayed on him while he cried. The report switched back to me saying something abstract and philosophical, and then it was over, leaving me staring at the screen, stunned.

CHAPTER FOURTEEN

Cruel and Unusual

When I arrived at Santa Rosa Correctional Institution in the town of Milton, Florida, I was escorted to a forty-by-forty-foot room where more than two dozen incarcerated men sat sadly while uniformed correctional staff buzzed in and out.

There were six-foot-tall metal cages in the corner that couldn't have been more than four feet by four feet. In all my years of visiting prisons, I had never seen such small cages used to hold a prisoner inside a secure prison. In one cage, wedged into the corner, sat a small man in a wheelchair. I couldn't see his face, but I felt certain it was the inmate I was there to see: Joe Sullivan.

The cage was so small that when the guards tried to remove his wheelchair, they couldn't budge it. They tugged at the chair with loud grunts and tried to force it free, but it was completely stuck.

I could hear Joe crying. He occasionally made a whining

sound, and his shoulders jerked up and down. When the staff proposed turning the cage on its side, he moaned audibly. Two inmate trusties lifted and tilted the heavy cage, while three officers yanked Joe's chair with a violent pull that finally dislodged it. The guards gave each other high fives, the inmate trusties walked away silently, and Joe sat motionless in his chair in the middle of the room, looking down at his feet.

I walked over to him and introduced myself. His face was tearstained, and his eyes were red, but he looked up at me and began clapping his hands giddily. "Yeah! Yeah! Mr. Bryan." He smiled and offered me both of his hands, which I took.

I wheeled Joe to a cramped office for our legal visit. Despite the terrifying start to the visit, he was extremely cheerful. I couldn't shake the feeling that I was talking to a young child.

At the time of his arrest in 1989, Joe Sullivan was a thirteen-year-old boy with mental disabilities who had suffered severe neglect and abuse from his father. Two older boys had convinced him to help them burgle the home of an older woman. The day of the burglary, the woman was also brutally sexually assaulted in her home. Joe admitted helping the older boys with the burglary earlier in the day but adamantly denied any knowledge of or involvement in the rape. In spite of the lack of evidence against him, Joe was convicted as an adult and sentenced to life without parole.

I explained to Joe how disappointed we were that the State had destroyed the biological evidence that might have allowed us to prove he was innocent through DNA testing. We had discovered that both the victim and one of his codefendants had died. The other codefendant would not say anything about what had really happened, making it extremely difficult for us to challenge Joe's conviction. I then offered our new idea about challenging his sentence as unconstitutionally cruel and unusual punishment, which might create another way for him to possibly go home. He smiled throughout my explanation, although it was clear he didn't understand all of it.

We knew that filing a petition nearly twenty years after Joe's sentencing would be difficult, but laws had changed in that time. In 2005, the Supreme Court recognized that differences between children and adults required different levels of punishment, and the death penalty for juveniles was banned under the Eighth Amendment.

My staff and I wanted to take this positive development a step further: we wanted to challenge juvenile life-without-parole sentences.

Across the country, we filed similar challenges to life-without-parole sentences in several other cases, including Ian Manuel's in Florida, Trina Garnett's in Pennsylvania, and Antonio Nuñez's in California.

We filed cases in Alabama, including one for Evan Miller, a fourteen-year-old condemned to die in prison in Alabama. Evan is from a poor white family in North Alabama. His difficult life was punctuated by suicide attempts that started when he was in elementary school. His parents were abusive and had drug addiction problems, and he had been in and out of foster care. A middle-aged neighbor, Cole Cannon, had come over one night seeking to buy drugs from Evan's mother. The fourteen-year-old Evan and his sixteen-year-old friend went to the man's house with him to play cards. Cannon gave the teens drugs and played drinking games with them. At one point, he sent the boys out to buy more drugs. The boys returned and stayed over as it got later and later. Eventually, the boys thought Cannon had passed out and tried to steal his wallet. Cannon was startled awake and jumped on Evan. The other boy responded by hitting the man in the head with a bat. Both boys started beating him and then set his trailer on fire. Cole Cannon died, and Evan and his friend were charged with capital murder. The older boy made a deal with prosecutors and got a parole-eligible life sentence, while Evan was convicted and sentenced to life imprisonment without parole.

I got involved in Evan's case right after his trial and filed a motion to reduce his sentence, even though it was the mandatory punishment for someone convicted of capital murder who was too young to be executed. At a hearing, I asked the judge to reconsider Evan's sentence in light of his age. The prosecutor argued, "I think he should be executed. He deserves the death penalty." He then lamented that the law no longer authorized the execution of children because he just couldn't wait to put this fourteen-year-old boy in the electric chair and kill him. The judge denied our motion.

When I visited Evan at the jail, we would have long talks about sports and books, his family, music. We talked about all the things he wanted to do when he grew up. He once told me that a guard had punched him in the chest just because he had asked a question about meal times. He started crying as he told me this because he just couldn't understand why the officer had done that.

Evan was sent to the St. Clair Correctional Facility, a maximum-security adult prison. Not long after he first arrived, he was attacked by another prisoner, who stabbed him nine times. He recovered but was traumatized by the experience and disoriented by the violence. When he talked about his own act of violence, he seemed deeply confused about how it was possible he could have done something so destructive.

Most of the juvenile lifer cases we handled involved clients who shared Evan's confusion about their adolescent behavior. Many had matured into adults who were much more thoughtful and reflective; they were now capable of making responsible and appropriate decisions. They had all changed in some significant way and were now nothing like the confused children who had committed a violent crime.

I was sixteen years old, living in southern Delaware. I was headed outside one day, when our phone rang. My mother answered it as I strolled past her. A minute later I heard her scream inside the house. I ran back inside and saw her lying on the floor, sobbing, "Daddy, Daddy" while the phone's receiver dangled from its base. I picked it up; my aunt was on the line. She told me that my grandfather had been murdered.

My grandfather had for some time lived alone in the South Philadelphia housing projects. It was there that he was attacked and stabbed to death by several teens who had broken into his apartment to steal his black-and-white television set. He was eighty-six years old.

Our large family was devastated by his senseless murder. We all kept saying and thinking the same thing: *They didn't have to kill him.* There was no way an eighty-six-year-old man could have stopped them from getting away with their loot. My mother could never make sense of it. And neither could I. I knew kids at school who seemed out of control and violent, but still I wondered how someone could be so pointlessly destructive. My grandfather's murder left us with so many questions.

Now, decades later, I was starting to understand. In preparing litigation on behalf of the children we were representing, it was clear that these shocking and senseless crimes couldn't be evaluated honestly without understanding the lives these children had been forced to endure.

Generally considered to encompass ages twelve to eighteen, adolescence is defined by radical changes. There are the obvious and often distressing physical changes associated with puberty, but there is also an increased capacity for reasoned and mature judgment, impulse control, and autonomy.

Adolescents are still developing biologically and psychosocially, gaining life experience and background knowledge to inform their choices. The self-confidence needed to make reasoned judgments and stick by them is only just starting to kick in. Working on behalf of clients who had been tried as teenagers, we argued that neuroscience and new information about brain chemistry help explain the impaired judgment that teens often display. On top of the stresses all teens experience, those who grow up poor, or in environments marked by abuse, violence, dysfunction, neglect, and the absence of loving caretakers are left vulnerable to the sort of extremely poor decision-making that results in tragic violence.

We also argued that a death-in-prison sentence is—like the death penalty—an unchangeable, once-and-for-all judgment on the whole life of a human being that declares him or her forever unfit to be part of civil society. We asked courts to recognize that passing such a judgment on children below a certain age is not reasonable. They are human works in progress. Their potential for growth and change is enormous. Almost all of them will outgrow criminal behavior, and it is practically impossible to detect the few who will not.

We emphasized the hypocrisy of not allowing children to smoke, drink, vote, drive without restrictions, give blood, and buy guns because of their well-recognized lack of maturity and judgment while simultaneously treating some of the most at-risk, neglected, and impaired children exactly the same as full-grown adults in the criminal justice system.

In May 2009, the Supreme Court agreed to review Joe Sullivan's case and the case of Terrance Graham, a sixteen-year-old from Jacksonville, Florida, who had also been convicted of a non-homicide and sentenced to life with no parole. It felt like a miracle. There was a possibility that the court might create constitutional relief for all children sentenced to die in prison. Here was a thrilling chance to change the rules across the country.

When we filed our brief in the US Supreme Court, we were supported by national organizations including the American Psychological Association, the American Psychiatric Association, the American Bar Association, and the American Medical Association, as well as by former judges and prosecutors, social workers, civil rights groups, and human rights groups.

In November 2009, after the briefs were filed in Joe's case and the Graham case, I went to Washington for my third US Supreme Court oral argument. The court was packed, and national media was covering the case. A wide assortment of children's rights advocates, lawyers, and mental health experts was watching closely when we asked the court to declare life-without-parole sentences imposed on children unconstitutional.

During the argument, I told the court that the United

States is the only country in the world that imposes sentences of life imprisonment without parole on children—a practice that violates international law. We showed the court that these sentences are disproportionately imposed on children of color. We argued that these harsh punishments were created for adult criminals and were never intended for children. I also told the court that to say to any child of thirteen that he is fit only to die in prison is cruel.

I had no way of knowing if the court had been persuaded. Now all there was to do was wait.

CHAPTER FIFTEEN

Broken

Walter's decline came quickly. The moments of confusion got longer and longer. He started forgetting things he had done just a few hours earlier. The details of his business slipped away from him, which depressed him. At some point, I went over his records with him. He'd been selling things at a fraction of their worth and losing a lot of money.

His sister told me that he'd started wandering in the evenings and getting lost. He began drinking heavily, something he'd never done before. He told me that he was anxious all the time and that the alcohol calmed his nerves. Then one day he collapsed. He was at a hospital in Mobile when they reached me in Montgomery. I drove down to speak with his doctor, who told me that Walter had advanced dementia, likely trauma-induced, and that he would need constant care. The doctor also said the dementia would progress and that Walter's health would decline.

We met with Walter's family at our office and agreed that he should live with a relative who could care for him. After staying with one relative, he returned to Monroeville with his sister Katie Lee. For a while, he did much better there, but then his condition began to deteriorate again.

Soon, Walter needed to be moved into the sort of facility that provided care for the elderly and infirm. Most places wouldn't take him because he had been convicted of a felony. Even when we explained that he was wrongfully convicted and proved innocent, no one would admit him. Finally, EJI's social worker on staff, Maria Morrison, found a place in Montgomery that agreed to take Walter for a short stay—no longer than ninety days.

The whole thing made me incredibly sad and overwhelmed. Meanwhile, EJI's workload was increasing too quickly. I had just argued Joe Sullivan's case at the US Supreme Court and was anxiously awaiting that judgment. I was worried about the execution dates that were set for every other month in Alabama. I was worried about what the US Supreme Court would choose to do with all of the children condemned to die in prison. I was worried about whether EJI had enough staff and funding to take on all our cases. When I got to the Montgomery nursing home to see Walter a week after he'd arrived there, I felt like I had been worrying all day.

Walter sat in a common room with older, heavily medicated people watching TV. I stopped before I walked into the room and looked at him; he hadn't seen me yet. He looked sleepy and unhappy slumped in a reclining chair, his head resting on his hand. He was staring in the general direction of the television, but it didn't seem like he was watching the program. There was a sadness in his eyes I had never seen before. Looking at him, I felt my heart sink.

A nurse escorted me into the room. I walked up to Walter and put my hand on his shoulder. He stirred and looked up, then gave me a broad smile.

"Hey, there he is!" He sounded cheerful, and suddenly he looked like himself. He started laughing and stood up. I gave him a hug. I was relieved; he hadn't recognized some family members recently.

"How you doing?" I asked him while he leaned on me slightly.

"Well, you know, I'm doing okay," he replied cautiously. We started walking to his room where we could talk privately.

"Are you feeling better?" It was not a sensible question, but I was a little unnerved seeing Walter like this. He'd lost weight and he moved slowly, sliding his feet in his slippers across the floor. He grabbed my arm a few feet down the hall and leaned on me as we slowly made our way.

"Well, I told them people I got plenty of cars, plenty of cars." He spoke emphatically, with much more excitement than I'd heard from him in a while. "All different colors, shapes, and sizes. The man say, 'Your cars don't work.' I told him my cars do work, too." He looked at me. "You may have to talk to that man about my cars, okay?"

I nodded and thought of his field of metal. "You do have lots of cars—"

"I know!" He cut me off and started laughing. "See, I told them people, but they didn't believe me. I told them." He was smiling and chuckling now, but he looked confused. "Them people think I don't know what I'm talking about, but I know exactly what I'm talking about." He spoke defiantly. We reached his room, and he sat down on his bed while I pulled up a chair. He became still and quiet and suddenly looked very worried.

"Well, it looks like I'm back here," he said with a heavy sigh. "They done put me back on death row."

His voice was mournful.

"I tried, I tried, I tried, but they just won't let me be." He looked me in the eye. "Why they want to do somebody like they're doing me is something I'll never understand. Why are people like that? I mind my own business. I don't hurt nobody. I try to do right, and no matter what I do, people come along, put me right back on death row . . . for nothing. Nothing. I ain't done nothing to nobody. Nothing, nothing, nothing."

He was becoming agitated, so I put my hand on his arm.

"Hey, it's okay," I said as gently as I could. "It's not as bad as it seems. I think—"

"You're going to get me out, right? You're going to get me off the row again?"

"Walter, this isn't the row. You haven't been feeling well, and so you're here so you can get better. This is a hospital."

"They've got me again, and you've got to help me."

He was starting to panic, and I wasn't sure what to do. Then he started crying. "Please get me out of here. Please? They're going to execute me for no good reason, and I don't want to die in no electric chair." He was crying now with a forcefulness that alarmed me.

I moved to the bed next to him and put my arm around him. "It's okay, it's okay. Walter, it's going to be all right. It's going to be all right."

He was trembling, and I got up so that he could lie down. I began talking to him softly about trying to make arrangements so he could stay at home and how we needed to find help, and that the problem was that it really wasn't safe for him to be alone. I could see his eyes drooping as I spoke, and within a matter of minutes he was sound asleep. I pulled his blankets up. I'd been with him less than twenty minutes.

In the hallway, I asked one of the nurses how he'd been doing.

"He's really sweet," she said. "We love having him here. He's nice to the staff, very polite and gentle. Sometimes he gets upset and starts talking about prison and death row. We didn't know what he was talking about, but one of the girls looked him up on the Internet, and that's when we read what happened to him. Somebody said someone like that is not supposed to be here, but I told them that our job is to help anybody who needs help."

"Well, the State acknowledged that he didn't do anything wrong. He is innocent."

The nurse looked at me sweetly. "I know, Mr. Stevenson, but a lot of people here think that once you go to prison, whether you belong there or not, you become a dangerous person, and they don't want to have nothing to do with you."

"Well, that's a shame." It was all I could muster.

I left the facility shaken and disturbed. My cell phone rang as soon as I stepped outside. The Alabama Supreme Court had just scheduled another death row execution, for a prisoner named Jimmy Dill. I called Randy Susskind, EJI's deputy director and an outstanding litigator, to discuss what we would do to block the execution. We both knew that it was going to be difficult at this stage.

By 1999, news coverage of all the innocent people wrongly convicted had influenced a decline in the death-sentencing rate. But the terrorist attacks in New York City on September 11, 2001, and threats of terrorism seemed to disrupt the progress. People were afraid and clamping down on perceived threats with extreme punishments. But then a few years later, rates of execution and death sentencing were once again decreasing, and by 2010, the number of annual executions fell to less than half the number in 1999. New Jersey, New York,

Illinois, New Mexico, Connecticut, and Maryland all took capital punishment off the books. Alabama's death-sentencing rate had also dropped from the late 1990s, but it was still the highest in the country. By the end of 2009, Alabama had the nation's highest execution rate per capita.

Every other month, someone was facing execution, and we were scrambling to keep up. We were representing children sentenced to life without parole all over the country—South Dakota, Iowa, Michigan, Missouri, Arkansas, Virginia, Wisconsin, and California, as well as Mississippi, Georgia, North Carolina, Florida, and Louisiana.

In a two-week period, I visited Antonio Nuñez at a remote California prison and argued his case in an appellate court, while *also* actively trying to win relief for Trina Garnett in Pennsylvania and both Ian Manuel and Joe Sullivan in Florida. Prison officials weren't allowing Joe to have regular access to his wheelchair, and he had fallen repeatedly and injured himself. Ian was still in solitary. Trina's medical condition was worsening.

And, of course, our Alabama docket had never been more demanding. I was having an increasingly difficult time managing it all. At the same time, Walter moved back home, where his sister would do the best she could to take care of him. It was a worrisome situation for him and his family, for all of us.

By the time Jimmy Dill was scheduled for execution in Alabama, the entire EJI staff was exhausted. The execution date couldn't have come at a more difficult time. We had no prior involvement in Mr. Dill's case, which meant getting up to speed in the thirty days before his scheduled execution. It was an unusual crime. Mr. Dill was accused of shooting someone during the course of a drug deal after an argument erupted. The shooting victim did not die; Mr. Dill was arrested and charged with aggravated assault. He was in jail for nine months awaiting trial while the victim was released from the hospital and was recovering fine. But after several months of caring for him at home, the victim's wife apparently abandoned him and he became gravely ill and died. State prosecutors charged Mr. Dill with capital murder.

Jimmy Dill suffered from an intellectual disability and had been sexually and physically abused throughout his childhood. He'd struggled with drug addiction. And his appointed counsel did very little to prepare the case for trial.

No court had reviewed critical issues about the reliability of his conviction and sentence. Capital murder requires an intent to kill, but there was a persuasive argument that Jimmy had *not* intended to kill in this case—and that poor health care had caused the victim's death. Most gunshot victims don't die nine months later. It was surprising that the State was seeking the death penalty here. And the US Supreme Court had previously banned the execution of people with intellectual disability, so Mr. Dill should have been shielded from the death penalty, but no one had investigated or presented evidence in support of the claim.

Along with his other challenges, Mr. Dill had enormous difficulty speaking. He had a speech impediment that caused him to stutter badly, especially when he was excited or agitated. Because he had not previously had a lawyer who would see him or speak to him, Mr. Dill saw our intervention as something of a miracle. I sent my young lawyers to meet with him regularly after we got involved, and Mr. Dill called me frequently.

Once a condemned prisoner has completed the appeals process the first time, courts are deeply resistant to reviewing claims. Although I knew the odds were against us, Mr. Dill's severe disabilities had made me privately hopeful that maybe a judge would be concerned and at least let us present additional evidence. But every court told us, "Too late."

On the day of the scheduled execution, I once again found myself talking to a man who was about to be strapped down and killed. I had asked Mr. Dill to call throughout the day because we were waiting to hear the outcome of our final stay request at the US Supreme Court. Early in the day, he had sounded anxious, but he told me he wasn't going to give up hope. He tried to express his gratitude for what we had done in the weeks leading up to his execution. We had located family members with whom he had reconnected. We told him that we believed that he had been unfairly convicted and sentenced. Our efforts seemed to help him cope.

But then the Supreme Court denied our final request for a

stay of execution, and there was nothing else to do. He would be executed in less than an hour, and it was up to me to tell him that the court would not grant him a stay. I felt overwhelmed.

We spoke on the phone shortly before he was taken into the execution chamber. He was stuttering worse than usual. I sat for a long time holding the phone while he strained to speak. It was heartbreaking. Then, suddenly, I remembered something I had completely forgotten until that moment.

When I was a boy, my mother took me to church. One day, when I was about ten years old, I was outside the church with my friends. One of them had brought a relative who was visiting, a shy, nervous boy, to the service. I asked the visitor where he was from, and when this child tried to speak, he stumbled horribly. He had a severe speech impediment and couldn't even say the name of the town where he lived. I had never seen someone stutter like that; I thought he must have been joking or playing around, so I laughed. My friend looked at me worriedly, but I didn't stop. Out of the corner of my eye, I saw my mother looking at me with an expression I'd never seen before. It was a mix of horror, anger, and shame. It stopped my laughing instantly. I'd always felt adored by my mom, so I was unnerved when she called me over.

She was furious. "What are you doing?"

"What? I didn't do . . ."

"Don't you *ever* laugh at someone because they can't get their words out right. Don't you *ever* do that!"

"I'm sorry." I was devastated to be reprimanded by my mom so harshly. "Mom, I didn't mean to do anything wrong."

"You should know better, Bryan."

"I'm sorry. I thought . . ."

"I don't want to hear it, Bryan. There is no excuse, and I'm very disappointed in you. Now, I want you to go back over there and tell that little boy that you're sorry."

"Yes, ma'am."

"Then I want you to give that little boy a hug."

"Huh?"

"Then I want you to tell him that you love him." I looked up at her and, to my horror, saw that she was dead serious.

"Mom, I can't go over and tell that boy I love him. People will—" She gave me that look again. I somberly turned around and returned to my group of friends. They were all staring at me. I went up to the little boy who had struggled to speak.

"Look, man, I'm sorry," I said sincerely.

I looked over at my mother, who was still staring at me. I lunged at the boy to give him a very awkward hug. I think I startled him by grabbing him like that, but when he realized that I was trying to hug him, his body relaxed and he hugged me back.

My friends looked at me oddly as I spoke.

"Uh . . . also, uh . . . I love you!" I half smiled as I spoke. It made me feel less weird to just act like it was a joke. But then the boy hugged me tighter and whispered in my ear. He spoke flawlessly, without a stutter and without hesitation.

"I love you, too." There was such tenderness and earnestness in his voice, and just like that, I thought I would start crying.

I was in my office, talking to Jimmy Dill on the night of his execution, and I realized I was thinking about something that had happened nearly forty years earlier. I also realized that I was crying. The tears were sliding down my cheeks, runaways that escaped when I wasn't paying attention. Mr. Dill was still laboring to get his words out, desperately trying to thank me for trying to save his life. The guards were making noise behind him, and I could tell he was upset that he couldn't get his words out right, but I didn't want to interrupt him. So I sat there and let the tears fall down my face.

The harder he tried to speak, the more I wanted to cry. The long pauses gave me too much time to think. He would never have been convicted of capital murder if he had just had the money for a decent lawyer. He would never have been sentenced to death if someone had investigated his past. It all felt tragic. *Why couldn't they see it, too?* The Supreme Court had banned executing people with intellectual disabilities, but states like Alabama refused to assess who was actually disabled. We're supposed to sentence people fairly after fully considering their life circumstances. Instead, we exploit those who are unable to afford the legal assistance they need. There is no excuse for trying to kill them with less resistance.

On the phone with Mr. Dill, I thought about all of his struggles, all the terrible things he'd gone through and how his disabilities had broken him. There was no excuse for him to have shot someone, but it didn't make sense to kill him. I began to get angry about it. Why do we want to kill all the broken people? What is wrong with us, that we think a thing like that can be right?

I tried not to let Mr. Dill hear me crying. He finally got his words out.

"Mr. Bryan, I just want to thank you for fighting for me. I thank you for caring about me. I love y'all for trying to save me."

When I hung up the phone that night, I had a wet face and a broken heart. The lack of compassion I witnessed every day had finally exhausted me. I looked around my crowded office, at the stacks of records and papers, each pile filled with tragic stories, and I suddenly didn't want to be surrounded by all this anguish and misery. As I sat there, I thought myself a fool for having tried to fix situations that were so fatally broken. *It's time to stop. I can't do this anymore.*

For the first time, I realized that my life was full of brokenness. I worked in a broken system of justice. My clients were broken by mental illness, poverty, and racism. They were torn apart by disease, drugs and alcohol, pride, fear, and anger. I thought of Joe Sullivan and of Trina, Antonio, Ian, and dozens of other broken children we worked with, struggling to survive in prison. I thought of people broken by war, like Herbert Richardson; people broken by poverty, like Marsha Colbey; people broken by disability, like Avery Jenkins. In their broken state, they were judged and punished by people whose commitment to fairness had been broken by cynicism, hopelessness, and prejudice.

I looked at my computer and at the calendar on the wall. I looked again around my office at the stacks of files. I saw the list of our staff, which had grown to nearly forty people. And before I knew it, I was talking to myself aloud: "I can just leave. Why am I doing this?"

It took me a while to sort it out, but I realized something sitting there while Jimmy Dill was being killed at Holman prison. After working for more than twenty-five years, I understood that I don't do what I do because it's required or necessary or important. I don't do it because I have no choice.

I do what I do because I'm broken, too.

My years of struggling against inequality, abusive power, poverty, oppression, and injustice had finally revealed something to me about myself. Being close to suffering, death, and cruel punishments didn't just illuminate the brokenness of others; in a moment of anguish and heartbreak, it also exposed my own brokenness. You can't effectively fight abusive power, poverty, inequality, illness, oppression, or injustice and not be broken by it.

We are all broken by something. We have all hurt someone and have been hurt. We all share the condition of brokenness even if our brokenness is not equivalent. I desperately wanted mercy for Jimmy Dill and would have done anything to create justice for him, but I couldn't pretend that his struggle was disconnected from my own. The ways in which I have been hurt—and have hurt others—are different from the ways Jimmy Dill suffered and caused suffering. But our shared brokenness connected us.

I guess I'd always known but never fully considered that being broken is what makes us human. We all have our reasons. Sometimes we're fractured by the choices we make; sometimes we're shattered by things out of our control. But our brokenness is also the source of our common humanity, the basis for our shared search for comfort, meaning, and healing. Our shared vulnerability and imperfection is what gives us each our capacity for compassion.

We have a choice. We can embrace our humanness, which means embracing our broken natures and the compassion that remains our best hope for healing. Or we can deny our brokenness, deny compassion, and, as a result, deny our own humanity.

I thought of the guards strapping Jimmy Dill to the gurney that very hour. I thought of the people who would cheer his death and see it as some kind of victory. I realized they were broken people, too, even if they would never admit it. So many of us have become afraid and angry. We've become so fearful and vengeful that we've thrown away children, discarded the disabled, and allowed the imprisonment of the sick and the weak—not because they are a threat to public safety or beyond rehabilitation, but because we think it makes *us* seem tough, less broken.

I thought of the victims of violent crime and the survivors of murdered loved ones, and how we've pressured them to recycle their anguish and give it back to the offenders we prosecute.

I thought of the many ways we've legalized vengeful and cruel punishments, how we've allowed our victimization to justify the victimization of others. But punishing the broken— whether it's by walking away from them or hiding them from sight—only ensures that they remain broken, and that we do, too.

I frequently had difficult conversations with clients who were struggling and despairing over their situations. Whenever things got really bad, and they were questioning the value of their lives, I would remind them that each of us is more than the worst thing we've ever done. I told them that if someone tells a lie, that person is not *just* a liar. If you take something that doesn't belong to you, you are not *just* a thief. Even if you kill someone, you're not *just* a killer. So I told myself that evening what I had been telling my clients for years. I am more than broken. In fact, there is a strength, a power even, in understanding brokenness. Embracing our brokenness creates a desire for mercy, and perhaps a need to show mercy to others, too. When you experience mercy, you begin to recognize the humanity that resides in each of us.

All of a sudden, I felt stronger. I began thinking about what would happen if we all just acknowledged our brokenness, if we owned up to our weaknesses, our shortcomings, our biases, our fears. Maybe if we did, we wouldn't want to kill the broken among us who have killed others. Maybe we would look harder for solutions to caring for the disabled, the abused, the neglected, and the traumatized. If we acknowledged our brokenness, perhaps we would no longer take pride in mass incarceration, in executing people, in treating our most vulnerable peers with indifference.

I looked at the clock. It was 6:30 p.m. Mr. Dill was dead by now. I was very tired, and it was time to stop all this foolishness about quitting. It was time to be brave.

As I slowly made my way home, I understood that even as we are caught in a web of hurt and brokenness, we're also in a web of healing and mercy. I thought of the little boy with the stutter who hugged me outside of church, creating reconciliation and love. I didn't deserve reconciliation or love in that moment, but that's how mercy works. The power of just mercy is that it belongs to the undeserving. It's when mercy is least expected that it's most powerful—strong enough to break the cycle of victimization and victimhood, retribution and suffering. It has the power to heal the psychic harm and injuries that lead to aggression and violence, abuse of power, mass incarceration.

I left the office broken and brokenhearted about Jimmy Dill.

But I knew I would come back the next day. There was more work to do.

CHAPTER SIXTEEN

The Stonecatchers' Song of Sorrow

On May 17, 2010, I was sitting in my office waiting anxiously, when the US Supreme Court announced its decision: sentences of life imprisonment without parole imposed on children convicted of non-homicide crimes is cruel and unusual punishment and constitutionally impermissible.

My staff and I jumped up and down in celebration. Moments later we were flooded with calls from media, clients, families, and children's rights advocates. It was the first time the court had issued a categorical ban on a punishment other than the death penalty. I thought of my clients: Joe Sullivan was entitled to relief. Scores of people, including Antonio Nuñez and Ian Manuel, were entitled to reduced sentences.

Two years later, in June 2012, we celebrated another major victory for incarcerated juveniles. The Supreme Court had agreed to review Evan Miller's case and the case of a client from Arkansas, Kuntrell Jackson. The outcome? A constitutional ban on mandatory life-without-parole sentences

244 · JUST MERCY

imposed on children convicted of homicides. This meant that no child accused of *any* crime could ever again be automatically sentenced to die in prison.

There were more than two thousand condemned people who had been sentenced as children to life imprisonment without parole—now they were potentially eligible for relief and reduced sentences. Across the country, many prosecutors resisted retroactively applying the court's decision in *Miller v. Alabama* to old cases, but everyone now had new hope, including Trina Garnett.

We continued our work on issues involving children by pursuing more cases. I believe that no child under the age of eighteen should be housed with adults in jails or prisons. We filed cases seeking to stop the practice. I am also convinced that very young children should never be tried in adult court. No child of twelve, thirteen, or fourteen can defend him- or herself in the adult criminal justice system. Wrongful convictions and illegal trials involving young children are too common.

I was encouraged by the fact that nationwide the rate of mass incarceration was finally slowing down. For the first time in close to forty years, the country's prison population did not increase in 2011. In 2012, the United States saw the first decline in its prison population in decades.

Our death penalty work had also taken a hopeful turn.

We'd won relief for one hundred death row prisoners in Alabama. In 2013, the state recorded the lowest number of new death sentences since the mid-1970s. These were very hopeful developments.

We were able to finally launch the race and poverty initiative I'd long been hoping to start at EJI. For years I'd wanted to start a project to change the way we talk about racial history and how it informs contemporary race issues. We started working with poor children and families in Black Belt counties across the South. We brought hundreds of high school students to our office for fascinating discussions about rights and justice. Also, we worked on reports and materials to deepen the national conversation about the legacy of slavery and lynching and our nation's history of racial injustice.

I found the new race and poverty work extremely energizing. It closely connected to our criminal justice work; so much of our worst thinking about justice is steeped in the myths of racial difference. I believe that there are four institutions in American history that have shaped our approach to race and justice but remain poorly understood:

The first, of course, is slavery—and the second is the reign of terror against people of color that followed the collapse of Reconstruction through World War II. Older people of color in the South would occasionally come up to me after speeches to complain about how antagonized they feel when they hear news commentators talking about how 9/11 was the first act of domestic terrorism in America.

An older African American man once said to me, "You make them stop saying that! We grew up with terrorism all the time. The police, the Klan, anybody who was white could terrorize you. We had to worry about bombings and lynchings, racial violence of all kinds."

The racial terrorism of lynching in many ways created the modern death penalty. America's embrace of speedy executions was, in part, an attempt to redirect the violence of lynching while assuring white Southerners that black men would still pay the ultimate price.

Another practice that is not well known to most Americans is *convict leasing*. Convict leasing was introduced at the end of the nineteenth century to criminalize former slaves and convict them of nonsensical offenses so that freed men, women, and children could be "leased" to businesses and effectively forced back into slave labor. Private industries throughout the country made millions of dollars with free convict labor, while thousands of African Americans died in horrific work conditions. The practice of re-enslavement was so widespread in some states that it was characterized in a Pulitzer Prize–winning book by Douglas Blackmon as *Slavery by Another Name*.

Racial terror and the constant threat created by violently enforcing racial hierarchy were profoundly traumatizing for African Americans, creating all kinds of psychosocial distortions and difficulties that still manifest themselves today.

The third institution, "Jim Crow," is the legalized racial

segregation and suppression of basic rights that defined America from 1876 through 1965. It is more recent and is recognized in our national consciousness, but it is still not well understood. It seems to me that we've been quick to celebrate the achievements of the civil rights movement and slow to recognize the lasting damage of marginalization and subordination done in that era.

The legacy of racial profiling carries many of the same complications. Once I was preparing to do a hearing in a trial court in the Midwest and was sitting at the counsel table in an empty courtroom before the hearing. I was wearing a dark suit, white shirt, and tie. The judge and the prosecutor entered through a door in the back of the courtroom, laughing and chatting.

When the judge saw me sitting at the defense table, he said to me harshly, "Hey, you shouldn't be in here without counsel. Go back outside and wait in the hallway until your lawyer arrives."

I stood up and smiled broadly. I said, "Oh, I'm sorry, Your Honor, we haven't met. My name is Bryan Stevenson. I am the lawyer on the case set for hearing this morning."

The judge laughed at his mistake, and the prosecutor joined in. I forced myself to laugh because I didn't want my young client, a white child who had been prosecuted as an adult, to be disadvantaged by a conflict I had created with the judge before the hearing. But I was disheartened by the experience. Of course innocent mistakes occur, but constantly being underestimated, suspected, accused, watched, doubted, distrusted, presumed guilty, and even feared is a burden borne by people of color that can't be understood or confronted without a deeper conversation about our history of racial injustice.

The fourth institution is mass incarceration. Going into any prison is deeply confusing if you know anything about the racial demographics of America. The extreme overrepresentation and disproportionate sentencing of racial minorities, the targeted prosecution of drug crimes in poor communities, the criminalization of new immigrants and undocumented people, the political consequences of disenfranchising black voters—essentially, denying black people the right to vote, and the barriers to reentering the world after incarceration can only be fully understood through the lens of our racial history.

It was gratifying to be able, finally, to address some of these issues with young people and the community. I became hopeful that together, we might be able to push back against the suppression of this difficult history of racial injustice.

A bigger staff, bigger cases, and a bigger docket also sometimes meant bigger problems. While exciting and very gratifying, enforcing the Supreme Court's ruling banning life-without-parole sentences for children convicted of non-homicides was proving much more difficult than I had hoped.

Some judges seemed to want to get as close to life expectancy or death as possible before they would release child offenders. For example, Antonio Nuñez's judge in Orange County, California, replaced his sentence of life imprisonment without parole with a sentence of 175 years. I had to go back to an appellate court in California and argue to get that sentence replaced with something reasonable. We met resistance in Joe Sullivan's and Ian Manuel's cases as well. Ultimately, we were able to get sentences that meant they could both be released after serving a few more years.

In some cases, clients had already been in prison for decades and had very few, if any, support systems to help them reenter society. We decided to create a reentry program specifically for people who have spent many years in prison after being incarcerated when they were children. We would offer services, housing, job training, life skills, counseling, and anything else people coming out of prison needed to succeed. We told the judges and parole boards we were committed to providing the assistance our clients required.

In particular, the Louisiana clients serving life without parole for non-homicides faced many challenges. We undertook representation of all sixty of those eligible for relief. Almost all of them were at Angola, a notoriously difficult place to do time. Angola—a plantation before the end of the Civil War—forced inmates to work in the fields picking cotton. Prisoners were required to do manual labor in very difficult work environments or face solitary confinement or other discipline. It was not uncommon for inmates to be seriously injured, losing fingers or limbs, after working long hours in brutal and dangerous conditions. For years, prisoners who refused would receive "write-ups" that went into their files and would face months of solitary confinement.

We decided to prioritize resentencing hearings for the "old-timers," juvenile lifers who had been at Angola prison for decades. Joshua Carter and Robert Caston were the first two cases we decided to litigate. Mr. Carter had been in prison for fifty years. There, he developed glaucoma and didn't get the medical care he needed; he lost his sight in both eyes. Mr. Caston had been at Angola for forty-five years. He lost several fingers working in a prison factory and was now disabled as a result of his forced labor at Angola.

I traveled back and forth between the trial courts in Orleans Parish quite a bit on the Carter and Caston cases. The Orleans Parish courthouse is a massive structure with intimidating architecture. There are multiple courtrooms aligned down an enormous hallway with grand marble floors and high ceilings. Hundreds of people crowd the hallways, bustling between the various courtrooms each day. Hearings in the vast courthouse are never reliably scheduled. Frequently, there would be a date and time for the Carter and Caston resentencings, but it seemed to mean very little to anyone. I would arrive in court, and there would always be a stack of cases, and clients with lawyers gathered in an overcrowded courtroom, all waiting to be heard at the time of our hearings. Overwhelmed judges tried to manage the proceedings with bench meetings while dozens of young men—most of whom were black—sat handcuffed in standard jail-issued orange jumpsuits in the front of the court. Lawyers consulted with clients and family members scattered around the chaotic courtroom.

After three trips to New Orleans for sentencing hearings, we still did not have a new sentence for Mr. Carter or Mr. Caston. We met with the DA, filed papers with the judge, and consulted with a variety of local officials in an effort to achieve a new, constitutionally acceptable sentence. Because Mr. Carter and Mr. Caston had both been in prison for nearly fifty years, we wanted their immediate release.

There were two different judges and courtrooms involved, but we felt if we won immediate release for one, it might then become easier to win release for the other. Finally, it seemed we were close to success. After I made our arguments in the frenetic courtroom, the judge granted our motion. She detailed Mr. Caston's forty-five years at Angola for a non-homicide crime when he was sixteen. She noted that he had been sent to Angola in the 1960s. Then the judge pronounced a new sentence that meant Mr. Caston would be immediately released.

Then the people in the silent courtroom did something I'd never seen before: they erupted in applause. The defense lawyers, prosecutors, family members, and deputy sheriffs applauded. Other inmates waiting for their own cases to be addressed applauded in their handcuffs. Even the judge, who usually tolerated no disruptions, seemed to embrace the drama of the moment. Mr. Caston was overjoyed. He became the first person to be released as a result of the Supreme Court's ban on death-in-prison sentences for juvenile lifers.

We were thrilled—and ready for the next case. We went down the hall to Mr. Carter's courtroom. Mr. Carter had a large family who had maintained a close relationship with him despite the passage of time. His mother was nearly a hundred years old. She had vowed to Mr. Carter for decades that she wouldn't die until he came home from prison. To our great joy, we had another success, winning a new sentence that meant that he, too, would be released immediately. Mr. Carter's family was ecstatic. There were hugs and promises of home-cooked meals for me and the staff of EJI.

Exhausted, I wandered the halls of the courthouse, waiting for one more paper to be approved to clear the way for the release of Mr. Caston and Mr. Carter. That's when I noticed an older black woman sitting on the marble steps in the massive courthouse hallway. She had smooth dark skin, and I recognized her as someone who had been in the courtroom. I assumed that she was related or connected to one of the clients. She waved at me, gesturing for me to come to her.

When I walked over to her, she smiled at me. "Sit, sit. I want to talk to you," she said. She had a sweet voice that crackled.

I sat down beside her on the steps. "I've seen you here several times. Are you related to Mr. Caston or Mr. Carter?" I asked.

"No, no, no, I'm not related to nobody here. Not that I know of, anyway." She had a kind smile, and she looked at me intensely. "I just come here to help people. This is a place full of pain, so people need plenty of help around here."

"Well, that's really kind of you."

"No, it's what I'm supposed to do, so I do it." She looked away before locking eyes with me again. "My sixteen-year-old grandson was murdered fifteen years ago," she said, "and I loved that boy more than life itself."

I wasn't expecting that response and was instantly sobered. The woman grabbed my hand.

"I grieved and grieved and grieved. I asked the Lord why he let someone take my child like that. He was killed by some other boys. I came to this courtroom for the first time for their trials and sat in there and cried every day for nearly two weeks. None of it made any sense. Those boys were found guilty for killing my grandson, and the judge sent them away to prison forever. I thought it would make me feel better, but it actually made me feel worse."

She continued, "I sat in the courtroom after they were sentenced and just cried and cried. A lady came over to me and gave me a hug and let me lean on her. She asked me if the boys who got sentenced were my children, and I told her no. I told her the boy they killed was my child." She hesitated. "I think she sat with me for almost two hours. For well over an hour, we didn't neither one of us say a word. It felt good to finally have someone to lean on at that trial, and I've never forgotten that woman. I don't know who she was, but she made a difference."

"I'm so sorry about your grandson," I murmured. It was all I could think of to say.

"Well, you never fully recover, but you carry on, you carry on. I didn't know what to do with myself after those trials, so about a year later, I started coming down here. I don't really know why. I guess I just felt like maybe I could be someone, you know, that somebody hurting could lean on." She looped her arm with mine.

I smiled at her. "That's really wonderful."

"It has been wonderful. What's your name again?"

"It's Bryan."

"All these young children being sent to prison forever, all this grief and violence. Those judges throwing people away like they're not even human, people shooting each other, hurting each other like they don't care. It's a lot of pain. I decided that I was supposed to be here to catch some of the stones people cast at each other."

I chuckled when she said it. It reminded me of a talk I had given at a church meeting during the McMillian hearings. There were a few people in the African American community who withheld support of Walter, not because they thought he was guilty but because he had had an extramarital affair and wasn't active in the church. At the church meeting, I spoke mostly about Walter's case, but I also reminded people that when the woman accused of adultery was brought to Jesus, he told the accusers who wanted to stone her to death, "Let he who is without sin cast the first stone." Accusers retreated, and Jesus forgave. But today, our self-righteousness, our fear, and our anger have caused us to hurl stones at the people who fall down, even when we know we should forgive or show compassion. I told the congregation that we can't simply watch that happen. I told them we have to be stonecatchers.

When I chuckled at the older woman's invocation of the parable, she laughed, too. "I heard you in that courtroom today. I've even seen you here a couple of times before. I know you's a stonecatcher, too."

I laughed even more. "Well, I guess I try to be."

She put her arm around me and smiled back. "No, you done good today. I was so happy when that judge said that man was going home. It gave me goose bumps. Fifty years in prison, he can't even see no more."

She squeezed me a bit and then said, "Now, you keep this up and you're gonna end up like me, singing some sad songs." She paused and grew silent. I heard her chuckle before she continued. "But you keep singing. Your songs will make you strong. They might even make you happy."

People buzzed down the busy corridors of the courthouse while we sat silently.

When I finally excused myself, giving her a kiss on the cheek and telling her I needed to sign the prisoners' release papers, she stopped me. "Oh, wait." She dug around in her purse until she found a piece of wrapped peppermint candy. "Here, take this."

The gesture made me happy in a way that I can't fully explain.

"Well, thank you." I grinned appreciatively.

She waved at me, smiling. "Go on, go on."

Walter died on September 11, 2013. He remained kind and charming until the very end, despite his increasing confusion from the advanced dementia. He lived with his sister Katie, but in the last two years of his life, he couldn't enjoy the outdoors or get around much without help. One morning he fell and fractured his hip. The hospital sent him home with little hope of recovery. He lost a lot of weight and became less and less responsive to visitors. He passed away quietly in the night a short time later.

We held Walter's funeral at Limestone Faulk A.M.E. Zion Church near Monroeville on a rainy Saturday morning. It was the same pulpit where, more than twenty years earlier, I had spoken to the congregation about casting and catching stones. It felt strange to be back. People packed the church, and dozens more stood outside. I looked at the mostly poor, rural black people huddled together for this sad occasion, made all the more tragic by the unjustified pain and torment that had preceded it. I often had this feeling when I worked on Walter's case, that if the anguish of all of the oppressed people in Monroe County could be gathered in one place, it could power something extraordinary, capable of igniting some righteous disruption or transformational redemption.

The family had a large TV monitor near the casket that flashed dozens of pictures of Walter before the service. Almost all of the photos were taken on the day he was released from prison. Walter and I stood next to each other in several of the photos, and I was struck by how happy we both seemed. I sat in the church and watched the pictures with some disbelief about the time that had passed.

When Walter was on death row, he once told me how ill he had become during the execution of one of the men on his tier. "When they turned on the electric chair, you could smell the flesh burning! We were all banging on the bars to protest, to make ourselves feel better, but really it just made me sick. The harder I banged, the more I couldn't stand any of it."

He asked me once, "Do you ever think about dying? I never did before, but now I think about it all the time." He looked troubled. "This, right here, is a whole 'nother kind of situation. Guys on the row talk about what they're going to do before their executions, how they're going to act. I used to think it was crazy to talk like that, but I guess I'm starting to do it, too."

"Well, you should think about living, man—what you're going to do when you get out of here," I replied.

"Oh, I do that, too. I do that a lot. It's just hard when you see people going down that hall to be killed. Dying on some court schedule or some prison schedule ain't right. People are supposed to die on God's schedule."

The funeral service began. A choir sang. The preacher gave a rousing sermon that honored Walter, and lamented that he had been pulled away from his family in the prime of his life by lies and bigotry. I took the pulpit next, taking a deep breath before speaking. I told the congregation that Walter had become like a brother to me, that he was brave to trust his life to someone who was as young as I was then. I explained that we all owed Walter something. He had been threatened and terrorized, wrongly accused and wrongly condemned, but he never gave up. He survived the humiliation of his trial and the charges against him. He survived a guilty verdict, death row, and the wrongful condemnation of an entire state. While he did not survive without injury or trauma, he came out with his dignity. He had stood strong in the face of injustice—a strength that just might have made the rest of us a little safer, a little more protected from the abuse of power that had almost killed him. I suggested to his friends and family that Walter's strength, resistance, and perseverance were a triumph worth celebrating, an accomplishment to be remembered.

I felt the need to explain to people what Walter had taught me. Walter made me understand why we have to reform a system of criminal justice that continues to treat people better if they are rich and guilty than if they are poor and innocent. A system that favors wealth and status while denying the poor the legal help they need must be changed. Walter's case taught me that fear and anger are a threat to justice; they can infect a community, a state, or a nation and make us blind, irrational, and dangerous. I reflected on how mass imprisonment has littered the national landscape with monuments of reckless and excessive punishment and ravaged communities with our hopeless willingness to condemn and discard the most vulnerable among us.

I told the congregation that Walter's case had taught me that the death penalty is not about whether people deserve to die for the crimes they commit. The real question of capital punishment in this country is *Do we deserve to kill?*

Finally and most importantly, I told those gathered in the church that Walter had taught me that mercy is just when it is rooted in hopefulness and freely given. Mercy is most empowering, liberating, and transformative when it is directed at the undeserving. The people who haven't earned it, who haven't even sought it, are the most meaningful recipients of our compassion. Walter genuinely forgave the people who unfairly accused him, the people who convicted him, and the people who judged *him* unworthy of mercy. And in the end, it was just mercy toward others that allowed him to recover a life worth celebrating, a life that rediscovered the love and freedom that all humans desire, a life that overcame death and condemnation until it was time to die on God's schedule.

After the service, I didn't stay long. I walked outside and looked down the road and thought about the fact that no one was ever prosecuted for Ronda Morrison's murder after Walter's release. I thought about the anguish that must still create for her parents.

There were lots of people who came up to me who needed legal help for all sorts of things. I wrote my number down for each person and encouraged them to call my office. It made the journey home less sad to hope that maybe we could help.

Since the Supreme Court's 2012 ruling banning mandatory life imprisonment without parole for children, nearly two thousand people condemned to die in prison when they were children have been resentenced and now have a chance to go home. Nearly two hundred people previously sentenced to death in prison as juveniles have been released. More than a dozen of our Louisiana clients who were sentenced as juveniles to die in prison are now at home. Ian Manuel has been released. Antonio Nuñez has a chance to be released. And finally, Joe Sullivan has been released. Trina Garnett's sentence has been reduced and she is now eligible to be released. Her spirit remains strong.

I continue to meet stonecatchers along the way who inspire me and make me believe that we can do better than we've done for the accused, convicted, and condemned among us— as well as those who are victimized by crime and violence— and that all of us can do better for one another. The work continues.

ACKNOWLEDGMENTS

I want to thank the hundreds of accused, convicted, and imprisoned men, women, and children with whom I have worked and who have taught me so much about hope, justice, and mercy. I'm especially appreciative of and humbled by the people who appear in this book, victims and survivors of violence, criminal justice professionals, and those who have been condemned to unimaginably painful spaces and yet have shown tremendous courage and grace. All the names of people who appear in these pages are real with the exception of just a few whose privacy and security needed to be protected.

I want to thank Beverly Horowitz, Rebecca Gudelis, and the wonderful team at Delacorte Press and Random House Children's Books for their incredible assistance and guidance on this project. I am so honored to share my work with young people, whose understanding of these issues is crucial if we are to create a more just society. I want to thank Aaryn Urell and Randy Susskind at EJI for editing and feedback. I am also grateful to my agent, Doug Abrams, for his guidance. None of my work is possible without the extraordinary women and men who work at the Equal Justice Initiative. I'm proud to work with such talented and gifted people who strive each day to create a better world. Thank you, EJI.

NOTES

INTRODUCTION

14   **One in every fifteen people born . . .** Thomas P. Bonczar, "Prevalence of Imprisonment in the U.S. Population, 1974–2001," Bureau of Justice Statistics (August 2003), available at www.bjs.gov/index.cfm?ty=pbdetail&iid=836, accessed April 29, 2014.

14   **one in every three black male babies . . .** Bonczar, "Prevalence of Imprisonment"; "Report of The Sentencing Project to the United Nations Human Rights Committee Regarding Racial Disparities in the United States Criminal Justice System," The Sentencing Project (August 2013), available at http://sentencingproject .org/doc/publications/rd_ICCPR%20Race%20and%20Justice%20Shadow %20Report.pdf, accessed April 29, 2014.

15   **with more than a half million people . . .** "Fact Sheet: Trends in U.S. Corrections," The Sentencing Project (May 2012), available at www.sentencingproject.org/doc/ publications/inc_Trends_in_Corrections_Fact_sheet.pdf, accessed April 29, 2014; Marc Mauer and Ryan S. King, "A 25-Year Quagmire: The War on Drugs and Its Impact on American Society," *The Sentencing Project* (September 2007), 2, available at www.sentencingproject.org/doc/publications/dp_25yearquagmire .pdf, accessed April 29, 2014.

15   **We ban poor people . . .** Federal law bars states from providing SNAP benefits, formerly known as food stamps, to those who have been convicted of a drug-related felony, although states may opt out or modify this ban. Currently thirty-two states have some sort of ban based on prior drug convictions, including ten states that have permanent bans. States may also evict or deny individuals from receiving federal benefits related to housing assistance, whether through the Section 8 program or placement in public housing, based on drug convictions. Maggie McCarty, Randy Alison Aussenberg, Gene Falk, and David H. Carpenter, "Drug Testing and Crime-Related Restrictions in TANF, SNAP, and Housing Assistance," Congressional Research Service (September 17, 2013), available at www .fas.org/sgp/crs/misc/R42394.pdf, accessed April 29, 2014.

15   **Some states strip people . . .** Twelve states permanently disenfranchise all or some felony offenders. Thirty-five prohibit parolees from voting, and thirty-one prohibit those on probation from voting. The Sentencing Project, "Felony Disenfranchisement Laws in the United States" (June 2013), available at www.sentencingproject .org/publications/felony-disenfranchisement-laws-in-the-united-states/, accessed April 30, 2014.

15 **as a result, in several Southern states . . .** In Alabama, Mississippi, and Tennessee more than 10 percent of African Americans cannot vote. In Florida, Kentucky, and Virginia, more than one in five African Americans cannot vote. Christopher Uggen, Sarah Shannon, and Jeff Manza, "State-Level Estimates of Felon Disenfranchisement in the United States, 2010," The Sentencing Project (July 2012), available at http://sentencingproject.org/doc/publications/fd_State _Level_Estimates_of_Felon_Disen_2010.pdf, accessed April 30, 2014.

16 **Scores have been exonerated . . .** The Death Penalty Information Center reports that 144 death row inmates have been exonerated since 1973. "The Innocence List," Death Penalty Information Center, available at www.deathpenaltyinfo.org/ innocence-list-those-freed-death-row, accessed April 25, 2014.

16 **Hundreds of prisoners who are not . . .** According to the Innocence Project, there have been 316 post-conviction DNA exonerations in the United States. Eighteen of the exonerated prisoners spent time on death row. "DNA Exonerations Nationwide," The Innocence Project, available at www.innocenceproject.org/ Content/DNA_Exonerations_Nationwide.php, accessed April 25, 2014.

16 **Presumptions of guilt based on poverty . . .** John Lewis and Bryan Stevenson, "State of Equality and Justice in America: The Presumption of Guilt," *Washington Post* (May 17, 2013).

16 **Finally, we spend lots of money on prisons . . .** In 2010, the latest year for which statistics are currently available, the cost of incarceration in America was about $80 billion. Attorney General Eric Holder, American Bar Association Speech (August 12, 2013); Tracey Kyckelhahn and Tara Martin, Bureau of Justice Statistics, "Justice Expenditure and Employment Extracts, 2010–Preliminary" (July 2013), available at www.bjs.gov/index.cfm?ty=pbdetail&iid=4679, accessed April 30, 2014. By comparison, that figure was about $6.9 billion in 1980. Bureau of Justice Statistics, "Justice Expenditure and Employment Extracts—1980 and 1981 Data from the Annual General Finance and Employment Surveys" (March 1985), available at www.bjs.gov/index.cfm?ty=pbdetail&iid=3527, accessed April 30, 2014.

CHAPTER ONE: MOCKINGBIRD PLAYERS

26 **It wasn't until 1967 . . .** When the Virginia legislature passed the Racial Integrity Act in 1924, authorizing the forced sterilization of black women thought to be defective or dangerous and criminalizing marriage between a black person and white person, people in Caroline County took these pronouncements very seriously. Decades later, when a young white man, Richard Loving, fell in love with a black woman named Mildred Jeter, the young couple decided to get married after learning that Mildred was pregnant. They went to Washington, D.C., to "get legal," knowing that it wouldn't be possible in Virginia. They tried to stay away but

got homesick and returned to Caroline County after the wedding to be near their families. Word about the marriage got out, and some weeks later the sheriff and several armed deputies stormed into their home in the middle of the night to arrest Richard and Mildred for miscegenation. Jailed and humiliated, they were forced to plead guilty and were told that they should be grateful that their prison sentences would be suspended as long as they agreed to leave the county and not return for "at least twenty-five years." They fled the state again but this time decided to fight the law in court with a lawsuit filed with the assistance of the American Civil Liberties Union. In 1967, after years of defeats in lower courts, the U.S. Supreme Court struck down miscegenation laws, declaring them unconstitutional.

26   **Nearly a dozen people had been lynched . . .** The names of the people lynched are as follows: October 13, 1892: Burrell Jones, Moses Jones/Johnson, Jim Packard, and one unknown (brother of Jim Packard). Tuskegee University, "Record of Lynchings in Alabama from 1871 to 1920," compiled for the Alabama Department of Archives and History by the Tuskegee Normal and Industrial Institute, Alabama Dept. of Archives and History Digital Collections, available at http://digital.archives.alabama.gov/cdm/singleitem/collection/voices/id/2516, accesssed September 18, 2009; also, "Four Negroes Lynched," *New York Times* (October 14, 1892); Stewart Tolnay, compiler, "NAACP Lynching Records," Historical American Lynching Data Collection Project, available at http://people.uncw.edu/hinese/HAL/HAL%20Web%20Page.htm#Project%20HAL, accessed April 30, 2014.

> October 30, 1892: Allen Parker. Tuskegee University Archives; Tolnay,
>   "NAACP Lynching Records."
> August 30, 1897: Jack Pharr. Tuskegee University Archives; Tolnay,
>   "NAACP Lynching Records."
> September 2, 1897: Unknown. Tuskegee University Archives.
> August 23, 1905: Oliver Latt. Tuskegee University Archives.
> February 7, 1909: Will Parker. Tuskegee University Archives.
> August 9, 1915: James Fox. Tuskegee University Archives; "Negro
>   Lynched for Attacking Officer," *Montgomery Advertiser* (August 10,
>   1915). Tuskegee University Archives; Tolnay, "NAACP Lynching
>   Records."
> August 9, 1943: Willie Lee Cooper. "NAACP Describes Alabama's
>   Willie Lee Case as Lynching," *Journal and Guide* (September 8, 1943);
>   "NAACP Claims Man Lynched in Alabama," *Bee* (September 26,
>   1943); "Ala. Workman 'Lynched' After Quitting Job," *Afro-American*
>   (September 18, 1943). Tuskegee University Archives.
> May 7, 1954: Russell Charley. "Violence Flares in Dixie," *Pittsburgh
>   Courier* (June 5, 1954); "Suspect Lynching in Ala. Town," *Chicago
>   Defender* (June 12, 1954); "Hint Love Rivalry Led to Lynching,"

Chicago Defender (June 19, 1954); "NAACP Probes 'Bama Lynching," *Pittsburgh Courier* (June 26, 1954). Tuskegee University Archives.

CHAPTER TWO: STAND

35   **Suicide, prisoner-on-prisoner violence . . .** The Bureau of Justice Statistics reports that throughout the 1980s, several hundred incarcerated individuals died each year of suicide, homicide, and other "unknown" reasons. Christopher J. Mumola, "Suicide and Homicide in State Prisons and Local Jails," Bureau of Justice Statistics (August 2005), available at www.bjs.gov/index.cfm?ty=pbdetail&iid=1126, accessed April 30, 2014; Lawrence A. Greenfield, "Prisons and Prisoners in the United States," Bureau of Justice Statistics (April 1992), available at www.bjs.gov/index.cfm?ty=pbdetail&iid=1392.

41   **I found Bureau of Justice statistics . . .** In 1978, black people were eight times more likely than whites to be killed by police officers. Jodi M. Brown and Patrick A. Langan, "Policing and Homicide, 1976-1998: Justifiable Homicide by Police, Police Officers Murdered by Felons," Bureau of Justice Statistics (March 2001), available at www.bjs.gov/index.cfm?ty=pbdetail&iid=829, accessed April 30, 2014.

41   **the problem would get worse . . .** In states with "Stand Your Ground" laws, the rate of "justifiable" homicides of blacks more than doubled between 2005 and 2011, the period when the majority of these laws were enacted. The rate of such homicides against whites also rose, but only slightly, and the homicide rate against whites was much lower to begin with. "Shoot First: 'Stand Your Ground' Laws and Their Effect on Violent Crime and the Criminal Justice System," joint press release from the National Urban League, Mayors Against Illegal Guns, and VoteVets.org (September 2013), available at http://nul.iamempowered .com/content/mayors-against-illegal-guns-national-urban-league-votevets-release -report-showing-stand-your, accessed April 30, 2014.

CHAPTER THREE: TRIALS AND TRIBULATION

47   **"We're going to keep all of you" . . .** *McMillian v. Johnson,* Case No. 93-A-699-N, P. Exh. 12, Plaintiff's Memorandum in Opposition to Defendant's Motion for Summary Judgment (1994).

57   **In 1945, the Supreme Court upheld a Texas statute . . .** *Akins v. Texas,* 325 U.S. 398 (1945).

57   **Local jury commissions used statutory requirements . . .** David Cole, "Judgment and Discrimination," in *No Equal Justice: Race and Class in the American Criminal Justice System* (New York: New Press, 1999), 101–31.

57   **By the 1970s, the Supreme Court ruled** ... *Duren v. Missouri,* 439 U.S. 357 (1979); *Taylor v. Louisiana,* 419 U.S. 522 (1975).

58   **The practice of striking all** ... "Illegal Racial Discrimination in Jury Selection: A Continuing Legacy," Equal Justice Initiative (2009), available at www.eji.org/files/ EJI%20Race%20and%20Jury%20Report.pdf, accessed April 30, 2014.

CHAPTER SIX: SURELY DOOMED

84   **Alabama had more juveniles sentenced to death** ... Victor L. Streib, *Death Penalty for Juveniles* (Bloomington: Indiana University Press, 1987).

CHAPTER SEVEN: JUSTICE DENIED

109   **Court records revealed** ... *Giglio v. United States,* 405 U.S. 150 (1972); *Mooney v. Holohan,* 294 U.S. 103 (1935).

118   **The study conducted for that case** ... *McCleskey v. Kemp,* 481 U.S. 279, 286 (1987), citing David C. Baldus et al., "Comparative Review of Death Sentences: An Empirical Study of the Georgia Experience," *Journal of Criminal Law and Criminology 74* (1983): 661.

118   **In Alabama, even though 65 percent** ... American Bar Association, "Evaluating Fairness and Accuracy in State Death Penalty Systems: The Alabama Death Penalty Assessment Report" (June 2006), available at www.americanbar.org/ content/dam/aba/migrated/moratorium/assessmentproject/alabama/report .authcheckdam.pdf, accessed June 14, 2013.

118   **Black defendant and white victim pairings** ... *McCleskey v. Kemp,* 481 U.S. 286–87, citing Baldus et al., "Comparative Review"; U.S. General Accounting Office, *Death Penalty Sentencing: Research Indicates Pattern of Racial Disparities,* 1990, GAO/GGD-90-57 ("In 82 percent of the studies, race of victim was found to influence the likelihood of being charged with capital murder or receiving the death penalty, i.e., those who murdered whites were found to be more likely to be sentenced to death than those who murdered blacks").

CHAPTER EIGHT: ALL GOD'S CHILDREN

124   **Chester had extraordinarily high rates** ... The Chester Upland school district has in the past two decades often ranked as the worst in the Commonwealth of Pennsylvania. James T. Harris III, "Success amid Crisis in Chester," Philly.com (February 16, 2012), available at http://articles.philly.com/2012-02-16/news/31067474_1_school -district-curriculum-parents-and-guardians, accessed April 30, 2014.

124   **Nearly 46 percent . . .** In 2012, it was estimated by the Census Bureau that 45.6 percent of Chester's residents under the age of eighteen lived below the federal poverty level. U.S. Census Bureau, 2008–2012 American Community Survey, Chester city, Pennsylvania.

126   **Pennsylvania sentencing law was inflexible . . .** Until 2012, anyone convicted of first- or second-degree murder automatically received a sentence of life imprisonment without the possibility of parole. 18 Pennsylvania Consolidated Statutes § 1102; 61 Pennsylvania Consolidated Statutes § 6137. Life imprisonment without parole is possible, though no longer mandatory, for juveniles convicted of first- or second-degree murder. 18 Pennsylvania Consolidated Statutes § 1102.1.

127   **"This is the saddest case I've ever seen" . . .** Liliana Segura, "Throwaway People: Teens Sent to Die in Prison Will Get a Second Chance," *The Nation* (May 28, 2012).

127   **For a tragic crime committed at fourteen . . .** Segura, "Throwaway People"; *Commonwealth v. Garnett,* 485 A.2d 821 (Pa. Super. Ct. 1984).

127   **It wasn't until 2008 that most states . . .** The Federal Bureau of Prisons adopted a policy in 2008 that restricts the shackling of pregnant inmates. Federal Bureau of Prisons, "Program Statement: Escorted Trips, No. 5538.05" (October 6, 2008), available at www.bop.gov/policy/progstat/5538_005.pdf, accessed April 30, 2014. Currently twenty-four states have laws or policies that prevent or restrict the shackling of pregnant inmates or inmates giving birth. Dana Sussman, "Bound by Injustice: Challenging the Use of Shackles on Incarcerated Pregnant Women," *Cardozo Journal of Law and Gender* 15 (2009): 477; "State Standards for Pregnancy-Related Health Care and Abortion for Women in Prison," American Civil Liberties Union, available at www.aclu.org/maps/state-standards-pregnancy-related-health-care-and-abortion-women-prison-map, accessed April 28, 2014.

128   **She is one of nearly five hundred people . . .** Paula Reed Ward, "Pa. Top Court Retains Terms for Juvenile Lifers," *Pittsburgh Post-Gazette* (October 30, 2013); "Juvenile Life Without Parole (JLWOP) in Pennsylvania," Juvenile Law Center, available at http://jlc.org/current-initiatives/promoting-fairness-courts/juvenile-life-without-parole/jlwop-pennsylvania, accessed April 26, 2014.

128–129   **Juveniles housed in adult prisons . . .** In enacting the Prison Elimination Act of 2003, Congress found that juveniles in adult facilities are five times more likely to be sexually assaulted. 42 U.S.C. § 15601(4).

130   **As he sank deeper into despair . . .** Laughlin, "Does Separation Equal Suffering?"

130   **By 2010, Florida had sentenced . . .** Florida had sentenced a total of seventy-seven juveniles to life imprisonment without parole for non-homicide offenses. Brief of Petitioner, *Graham v. Florida,* U.S. Supreme Court (2009); Paolo G. Annino, David W. Rasmussen, and Chelsea B. Rice, *Juvenile Life without Parole for Non-Homicide Offenses: Florida Compared to the Nation* (2009), 2, table A.

131   **the youngest condemned children . . .** Two thirteen-year-olds in Florida, including

Joe Sullivan, had been sentenced to life imprisonment without parole for non-homicide offenses. Annino, Rasmussen, and Rice, *Juvenile Life without Parole for Non-Homicide Offenses,* chart E (2009).

131 **All of the youngest . . .** "Cruel and Unusual: Sentencing 13- and 14-Year-Old Children to Die in Prison," Equal Justice Initiative (2008), available at http://eji.org/eji/files/Cruel%20and%20Unusual%202008_0.pdf, accessed April 30, 2014.

131 **Florida had the largest population . . .** The United States is the only country in the world that sentences juveniles to die in prison for non-homicide offenses, and Florida has sentenced far more such offenders to life without parole than any other state. Annino, Rasmussen, and Rice, *Juvenile Life without Parole for Non-Homicide Offenses,* chart E.

132 **He got his hands on a gun . . .** *In re Nunez,* 173 Cal.App. 4th 709, 720–21 (2009).

134 **For instance, in the infamous . . .** James Goodman, *Stories of Scottsboro* (New York: Pantheon Books, 1994), 8.

134 **Influential criminologists predicted . . .** "Super-predator" language was commonly used in conjunction with dire predictions that a vast increase in violent juvenile crime was occurring or about to occur. See Office of Juvenile Justice and Delinquency Prevention, U.S. Department of Justice, "Juvenile Justice: A Century of Change" (1999), 4–5, available at www.ncjrs.gov/pdffiles1/ojjdp/178993.pdf, accessed April 30, 2014. See, for example, Sacha Coupet, "What to Do with the Sheep in Wolf's Clothing: The Role of Rhetoric and Reality About Youth Offenders in the Constructive Dismantling of the Juvenile Justice System," *University of Pennsylvania Law Review* 148 (2000): 1303, 1307; Laura A. Bazelon, "Exploding the Superpredator Myth: Why Infancy Is the Preadolescent's Best Defense in Juvenile Court," *New York University Law Review* 75 (2000): 159. Much of the frightening imagery was racially coded; see, for example, John J. DiIulio, "My Black Crime Problem, and Ours," *City Journal* (Spring 1996), available at www.city-journal.org/html/6_2_my_black.html, accessed April 30, 2014 ("270,000 more young predators on the streets than in 1990, coming at us in waves over the next two decades . . . as many as half of these juvenile super-predators could be young black males"); William J. Bennett, John J. DiIulio Jr., and John P. Walters, *Body Count: Moral Poverty—And How to Win America's War Against Crime and Drugs* (New York: Simon and Schuster, 1996), 27–28.

134–135 **Sometimes expressly focusing on black . . .** John J. DiIulio Jr., "The Coming of the Super-Predators," *Weekly Standard* (November 27, 1995), 23.

135 **The juvenile population in America increased . . .** See, for example, Elizabeth Becker, "As Ex-Theorist on Young 'Superpredators,' Bush Aide Has Regrets," *New York Times* (February 9, 2001), A19.

137 **We decided to publish a report . . .** "Cruel and Unusual."

CHAPTER NINE: I'M HERE

147 **"Me, I can simply look"** ... *McMillian v. Alabama,* CC-87-682.60, Testimony of Ralph Myers During Rule 32 Hearing, April 16, 1992.

CHAPTER TEN: MITIGATION

163 **In the 1960s and 1970s** ... In these decades, legislative and judicial reforms tightened the procedures by which individuals where subject to involuntary commitment. Stanley S. Herr, Stephen Arons, and Richard E. Wallace Jr., *Legal Rights and Mental Health Care* (Lexington, MA: Lexington Books, 1983). In 1978, the United States Supreme Court raised the burden on states seeking to have individuals involuntarily committed to mental health hospitals from the low "preponderance of the evidence" standard to a more difficult "clear and convincing evidence" standard. *Addington v. Texas,* 441 U.S. 418 (1978).

163 **Today, over 50 percent of prison** ... Doris J. James and Lauren E. Glaze, "Mental Health Problems of Prison and Jail Inmates," Special Report, Bureau of Justice Statistics (September 2006), available at http://bjs.gov/content/pub/pdf/mhppji .pdf, accessed July 2, 2013. This number breaks down to 56 percent percent of state prisoners, 45 percent of federal prisoners, and 64 percent of local jail prisoners. In total, that accounts for an estimated 1,264,300 inmates. This study is the most comprehensive recent study available and yet was conducted in 2005, so numbers may have changed in more recent years. However, current sources (2012–13) still cite this study, so I feel comfortable concluding that it is still the most comprehensive and up-to-date source on the subject.

163 **In fact, there are more than three** ... Torrey et al., "More Mentally Ill Persons," 1.

166 **In fact, it was in the 1950s** ... Alabama, Georgia, and South Carolina all began to fly the Confederate battle flag in symbolic opposition to the *Brown* decision. James Forman Jr., "Driving Dixie Down: Removing the Confederate Flag from Southern State Capitols," *Yale Law Journal* 101 (1991): 505.

CHAPTER ELEVEN: I'LL FLY AWAY

184 **Writers at local newspapers** ... Connie Baggett, "DA: TV Account of McMillian's Conviction a 'Disgrace,'" *Mobile Press Register* (November 24, 1992).

CHAPTER TWELVE: MOTHER, MOTHER

201 **In fact, nationwide, most women** ... "Case Summaries for Current Female Death Row Inmates." Death Penalty Information Center, available at www

.deathpenaltyinfo.org/case-summaries-current-female-death-row-inmates, accessed August 13, 2013.

201 **The criminalization of infant mortality** . . . This phenomenon of charging women, particularly poor women and women of color, who give birth to stillborn babies or children who live only a short time, now seems commonplace to a casual observer of current events. Michelle Oberman, "The Control of Pregnancy and the Criminalization of Femaleness," *Berkeley Journal of Gender, Law, and Justice* 7 (2013): 1; Ada Calhoun, "The Criminalization of Bad Mothers," *New York Times* (April 25, 2012).

202 **In time, the Alabama Supreme Court** . . . Ex parte Ankrom, 2013 WL 135748 (Ala. January 11, 2013); Ex parte Hicks, No. 1110620 (Ala. April 18, 2014).

203 **Approximately 75 to 80 percent** . . . Angela Hattery and Earl Smith, *Prisoner Reentry and Social Capital: The Long Road to Reintegration* (Lanham, MD: Lexington, 2010).

CHAPTER FIFTEEN: BROKEN

230 **But then a few years later, rates of execution** . . . "Facts About the Death Penalty." Death Penalty Information Center (May 2, 2013), available at www.deathpenaltyinfo.org/FactSheet.pdf, accessed August 31, 2013.

230 **by 2010, the number of annual executions** . . . There were 46 executions in 2010 compared to 98 in 1999. "Executions by Year Since 1976," Death Penalty Information Center, available at www.deathpenaltyinfo.org/executions-year, accessed April 29, 2014.

230–231 **New Jersey, New York, Illinois** . . . Act of May 2, 2013, ch. 156, 2013 Maryland laws; Act of April 25, 2012, Pub. Act No. 12-5, 2012 Connecticut Acts (Reg. Sess.); 725 Illinois Comp. Stat. 5/119-1 (2011); Act of March 18, 2009, ch. 11, 2009 New Mexico laws; Act of December 17, 2007, ch. 204, 2007 New Jersey laws.

231 **Alabama's death-sentencing rate** . . . "Alabama's Death Sentencing and Execution Rates Continue to Be Highest in the Country," Equal Justice Initiative (February 3, 2011), available at www.eji.org/node/503, accesssed August 31, 2013.

CHAPTER SIXTEEN: THE STONECATCHERS' SONG OF SORROW

243 **On May 17, 2010, I was sitting** . . . *Graham v. Florida,* 560 U.S. 48 (2010).

243 **Two years later, in June 2012** . . . *Miller v. Alabama,* 132 S. Ct. 2455 (2012).

245 **I believe that there are four institutions** . . . Alex Carp, "Walking with the Wind: Alex Carp Interviews Bryan Stevenson," *Guernica* (March 17, 2014), available at www.guernicamag.com/interviews/walking-with-the-wind, accessed April 30, 2014.

249 **I had to go back to an appellate court** . . . *People v. Nunez,* 195 Cal.App. 4th 404 (2011).

INDEX